Contents

Figures

page

Chapter 1

Introduction

American grand strategy is the collection of plans and policies by which the leadership of the United States mobilizes and deploys the country's resources and capabilities, both military and nonmilitary, to achieve its national goals. Grand strategy exists in the real world of governing whether it is carefully formulated and articulated in advance, or whether it evolves ad hoc out of world views, predilections, and subjectivities of those who govern. It is a fruitful field for scholars and students to study so that those who govern and those who are governed might have the richest conceptual repertoire with which to construct and evaluate national policies.[1]

As the quotation above explains, grand strategy, can either be carefully formulated, or can come about in an ad hoc manner, influenced heavily by the personalities and beliefs of those who govern. Intuitively, a carefully formulated grand strategy sounds more pragmatic and safer than one thrown together on an ad hoc basis. As dangerous as ad hoc grand strategy seems, there is an even more sinister alternative, one in which the employment of the nation's resources and capabilities are never brought together in a coordinated fashion. Instead, the resources and capabilities are used in ways that contradict each other, so much so, that the political objectives become unachievable.

The relatively short history of United States (US) involvement in the Middle East is full of frustrating set backs and lost opportunities whose origins can be traced to a lack of grand strategy for the region. Some examples that immediately spring to mind are the closure of the Suez Canal, the oil embargo, the failed peace processes, the Iranian hostage crisis, the Iran-Iraq war, and the rise of Islamic radicals. In each of these examples, the United States' inability to formulate a grand strategy, pre-planned or ad hoc, led to the failure of stated political objectives.

The US first became actively engaged in the Middle East in 1946, when President Harry Truman extended the policy of containment to cover the region, forcing the Soviet Union to abandon its expansion into Iran.[2] In 1957, President Dwight Eisenhower signed into law House Joint Resolution 117, which quickly became known as the Eisenhower Doctrine. The law stated, "The United States is prepared to use armed forces to assist any such nation or groups of nations [in the Middle East] requesting assistance against armed aggression from any country controlled by international communism."[3] In 1958, Eisenhower invoked this law when the Lebanese government asked US forces to intervene in Lebanon for the first time.[4] In 1970, President Richard Nixon affirmed the Eisenhower Doctrine by clearly articulating that the US had three strategic goals in the Middle East: prevent conflict which had the potential spill over into the entire region, continue the supply of oil to the West, and ensure the Suez Canal remained open to international trade.[5]

United States involvement in the Middle East is a fascinating topic simply because there are so many plots and subplots, that all impact any outcome US policy tries to achieve. As one Middle East scholar and former Army officer I interviewed told me:

> I was there as an Army major: in Beirut Jan-June 1984; and in southern Lebanon from July 1984 to March 1985. I went over thinking I knew a bit about the Middle East based on reading interests and a few courses I had taken here and there. I came back sure that I was a novice in the world of the Middle East—and I was. I certainly was no expert, nor did I meet any—then or since.[6]

Certainly, to be considered an expert, one would need a comprehensive understanding of all the issues that flow through the Middle East. These issues span thousands of years and involve complex interactions between religion, ethnicity, natural resources, foreign interventions, poverty, wealth, tribalism, and a myriad of other factors. To steal a line from Carl von Clausewitz, "an [understanding of the Middle East] that ignores any of them or seeks to fix an arbitrary relationship between them would conflict with reality to such an extent that for this reason alone it would be totally useless."[7]

Due to limits in length and the recognition, it is not possible to convey a true understanding of any of the major undercurrents of the Middle East in a single thesis. This paper seeks only to explain grand strategy formulation and execution from a US perspective. To do this, the case study method will be used to look at the US military intervention in Lebanon in 1982 to 1984 and the invasion of Iraq in 2003. The central question that this paper seeks to answer is "Did the US have a grand strategy in Lebanon from 1982 to 1983 and Iraq in 2003?" To achieve this goal, the paper will start in chapter 2 with ans introduction to grand strategy theory by Carl von Clausewitz and B.H. Liddell Hart. In addition, historians Eliot Cohen and Walter Russell Mead, argue that US actions in Lebanon and Iraq fit into a larger pattern of UUS Foreign Policy. Chapter 2 concludes with an analysis by Dennis Drew and Donald Snow of the components that should be part of any properly formulated grand strategy.

Chapter 3 explores the history of grand strategy implementation by the US. Of particular interest is the National Security Act of 1947, which changed how the government is organized to both formulate and execute grand strategy. The role of the National Security Counsel, National Security Advisor and the interagency process are discussed in terms of how they affect the formulation of grand strategy.

The case studies begin in Chapter 4 by looking at the United States Marine Corps intervention in Lebanon from 1982 to 1984. The case study starts with a brief historical overview and attempts to determine whether or not the US had a grand strategy by assessing four critical factors: Did the policy makers understand the need for implementing policies that would enhance political reconciliation as part of the larger grand strategy? Did those same policy makers understand that without political reconciliation, none of the other policies would lead to the achievement of the political objectives? Were the branches, cabinets, and agencies of the US government able to set aside their philosophical differences and parochial interests to form a coordinated and unified plan of action, or did their differences become so great they stopped supporting each other all together? Did the US maintain its stated goal of empowering the Lebanese to solve their own problems, or did the US "Americanize" the solution and thereby undercut their larger political objectives? Finally, were the actions the military was asked to take conducive to achieving the political objectives or did military action become counterproductive?

The Lebanon case study concludes by summarizing how the lack of grand strategy that allowed the US military to drift from its original role as peacekeepers, focused on evacuating the Palestinian Liberation Organization (PLO), to shelling Syrian positions with the USS New Jersey's 16-inch guns.

The second case study begins in chapter 5 and covers the US invasion of Iraq in 2003. This case study follows the same framework established in chapter 4 and uses the same four questions to analyze the role grand strategy played in progression of the US military mission from simply deposing Saddam Hussein to a full occupation of Iraq.

Finally, the conclusion summarizes the results and synthesizes the theory presented in chapter 3 with the case studies from chapters 4 and 5 to give the reader a full understanding of why all the instruments of national power were never brought to bear on the problems the US faced in both Lebanon and Iraq.

Notes

1. Duke University, "Duke University Program in American Grand Strategy," http://www.duke.edu/wed/agsp/#grandstrategy (accessed 22 May 2012).

2. John Collins, *Grand Strategy: Practices and Principles* (Annapolis, MD: Naval Institute Press, 1973), 149.

3. Peter Hahn, "Securing the Middle East: The Eisenhower Doctrine of 1957," *Presidential Studies Quarterly* 36, no. 1 (2006). The Eisenhower Doctrine of 1957 declared that the United States would distribute economic and military aid and, if necessary, use military force to stop the spread of communism in the Middle East. The doctrine consisted of a major commitment by the United States to the security and stability of the Middle East and signaled a new level of US resolve to exert influence in international affairs. By issuing the doctrine, Eisenhower raised the prospect that the United States would fight in the Middle East and accepted responsibilities in the region that the United States would retain for decades to come.

4. Roger Spiller, *Not War But Like War: The American Intervention in Lebanon,* (Fort Leavenworth, Combat Studies Institute, 1981), 2.

5. Collins, *Grand Strategy: Practices and Principles,* 151. The first goal was tied to balance of power and the global policy of containment. The second goal of continuing the supply of oil to the free world was not just for the US, but Europe and Japan were heavily dependent on Middle East Oil. The third goal was directly tied to the second goal, because most of the Middle East oil traveled through the Suez on its way to the West.

6. CB20120312C0001, ORHA Official, Interview by Charles Bris-Bois, 12 March 2012, Quantico. All interviews conducted for this research were done on the condition of anonymity and therefore names will not be released.

7. Michael Howard and Peter Paret, eds., *On War* (Princeton, NJ: Princeton University Press, 1984), 89.

Chapter 2
Grand Strategy, Doctrine, and Definitions

The sorry state of peace...that has followed most wars can be traced to the fact that, unlike strategy, the realm of grand strategy is for the most part terra incognita—still awaiting exploration, and understanding.[1]

—B.H. Liddell Hart, *Strategy*

To determine if the US applied the principles of grand strategy to the military interventions in Beirut and Iraq, we must first define what grand strategy is, what its components are, and how it is supposed to be developed, coordinated, and implemented. To accomplish this goal, the paper will build a theoretical foundation based on the works of Carl von Clausewitz and B.H. Liddell Hart. These theorists will be followed by two modern historians Walter Russell Mead and Eliot Cohen who will be used to help put Lebanon and Iraq into the larger historical context, where they can be seen as part of a larger continuum of US strategic policy. Finally, Dennis Drew and Donald Snow are used to explain how the modern US military, in theory, defines and formulates grand strategy.

Carl von Clausewitz

Carl von Clausewitz was a Prussian military officer and a scholar. As a soldier, he gained tremendous battlefield experience during the period of the Napoleonic wars, which he attempted to distill into a theory of war. The work he left, *On War*, although unfinished, has become one of the most influential books on the art of war ever written. Clausewitz wrote the majority of *On War* between 1815 and 1830. Highly influenced by the scholarly works of the enlightenment and German Romanticism, he endeavored to write principles of war that would last the test of time and would not become outdated by advances in technology and new tactics.[2] He intended the work to be more than just a rulebook for war. He wanted to provide soldiers and statesmen the tools needed to develop their own logic, using the laws and principles he laid out.[3] The most famous of these principles is his Remarkable Trinity. First, this trinity is composed of blind natural force of violence, hatred, and enmity. Second, the play of chance and probability, within which commanders are free to use their creativity. Finally, the third piece to the trinity was reason, meaning that war is subjugated to policy.[4] This last piece of the trinity, in which Clausewitz added that war is subordinate to policy, was not fully articulated until 1827.[5] Prior to 1827, Clausewitz's focus had primarily been on explaining war through the lens of the French Revolutionary and Napoleonic wars.[6] Russia's wars with Poland and the Ottoman Empire in the mid 1820s, forced him to rethink what he had written in chapters one through six of *On War*.[7] He came to the conclusion that the nature of war was not linear, meaning that wars did not always start small and expand.[8] The Russian wars convinced him that wars could be fought for limited purposes as well. Therefore, his position that "the complete or partial destruction of the enemy must be regarded as the sole object of all engagements" was no longer logically consistent.[9] He now recognized there were at least two types of war, one aimed at complete destruction of the enemy, in which the victor could dictate the terms of peace, and one in which you fight for limited objectives in order to secure a negotiated peace.[10] Thus, Clausewitz went back and added chapters seven and eight to *On War* with this new understanding and also revised chapters one and two. He intended to revise the remaining chapters, but he passed away in 1831 before he could complete the alterations.[11]

Hew Strachan, the Chichele Professor of War at Oxford University and perhaps the world's leading scholar on Clausewitz, contends that the fact *On War* was never finished is, "the very source of its enduring strength." Generation after generation has been able to take selectively from *On War* what they desired.[12] This includes those who advocate the need for grand strategy, even though Clausewitz never used the term.

It can be argued that the closest Clausewitz came to describing grand strategy was the way in which he described "policy." In a note he wrote in 1827, describing how he was revising his thoughts, Clausewitz contended that, "because there are two types of wars, it must lead to the recognition that war is a political act which is not wholly autonomous; a true political instrument that does not act on its own but is controlled by something else, the hand of policy."[13] The problem with this is that Clausewitz never truly defined what he meant by, policy.[14]

In German, the word *Politik* means both policy and domestic politics. In the Michael Howard and Peter Paret translation of *On War*, they chose to translate *Politik* to mean policy, similar in meaning to the modern use of the term foreign policy, completely ignoring the domestic political aspects.[15] Yet Clausewitz himself recognized the importance of domestic politics on strategy in Book 8, when he described how French internal politics in the 1790s transformed the wars of Napoleon.[16]

For Clausewitz, the importance of *Politik*, using both the foreign policy and domestic politics translation, was that it formed a unifying structure under which he could bring all forms of war together into a coherent explanation.[17] *Politik,* under Clausewitz's intentionally vague definition, became the "trustee of all the interest of the state," the "great outlines" upon which war was planned and carried out.[18] It did so by "unifying and reconciling all the aspects of internal administration as well as the spiritual values, and whatever else the moral philosopher may care to add."[19]

In order to maintain consistency in his logic, Clausewitz refused to enter into a debate about how policy unified and reconciled all the aspects of the internal administration. Instead, he dismissed this question by saying, "that it [policy], can err, subserve the ambitions, private interests, and vanity of those in power, is neither here nor there...here we can only treat policy as representative of all interests of the community."[20] Antulio Echevaria, a military practitioner, Princeton scholar, and head of the Strategic Studies Institute at the US Army War College, who has written extensively on strategy, claims that Clausewitz did this to avoid being bogged down in the details, however, the unintended effect was to deny that friction may exist in the formulation of policy as well as in the execution of war.[21] More significantly, it led to the assumption that policy is united around a single purpose, rather than several competing ones.[22]

This paper will endeavor to show that in Lebanon and Iraq, there were many competing policy interests, not one, and that the private interests and ambitions of those in power affected the development of a grand strategy. As discussed above, Clausewitz never employed the term grand strategy, but his concept that, policy, unifies and reconciles all the aspects of the internal administration is hugely important to any discussion on the topic. To the extent that this paper will use *On War* and Clausewitz's theories, it will be to prove that the US never established a grand strategy because it was unable to formulate a policy that was "representative of all interests of the community."

B.H. Liddell Hart

Liddell Hart was a British Army Officer and theorist who is best known for his ideas on mechanized warfare, mobility, and airpower.[23] Liddell Hart's view on grand strategy is that it should be used to ensure that war achieves a better peace for the victor when hostilities are complete. Liddell Hart said, "It is essential to conduct war with constant regard to the peace you desire."[24] Liddell Hart links this belief to Clausewitz's often quoted premise that, war is a continuation of policy by other means. In other words, the object of war is to achieve what diplomacy alone could not. War therefore, must always be conducted with the "subsequent peace" in mind.[25] For Liddell Hart, policy and grand strategy are separated by the fact that policy is "the object of the war, what is to be achieved;" while grand strategy is policy in action, "the [coordination and direction] of all the resources of a nation...towards the attainment of the political object of the war—the goal defined by the fundamental policy."[26] As a precursor to the modern United States' definition of instruments of national power, Liddell Hart stresses that grand strategy must go beyond military force and incorporate financial pressure, diplomatic pressure, and ethical pressure, "to weaken and opponent's will."[27] To accomplish this, grand strategy must include calculations of the resources required: money, manpower, and "moral resources" and a plan for how the government is going to ensure the resources exist in sufficient quantities.[28]

The case studies in chapters 4 and 5 will show that part of why the US failed to achieve its stated objectives in both Lebanon and Iraq, was because it failed to heed Liddell Hart's guidance. Liddell Hart believed grand strategy must include a properly formulated plan for marshaling appropriate levels of funding and manpower and then tying them to a strategy that combines military, diplomatic, and moral pressures in a holistic fashion.

The next section will attempt to provide a historical context for why it is so difficult for the US to coordinate and direct all the resources of the nation toward the attainment of the political objective.

Modern Theorists

Walter Russell Mead and Eliot Cohen will be used to expand on Clausewitz and Liddle Hart's, theoretical framework, or "High" theory of grand strategy, and help put the development of grand strategy in Lebanon and Iraq in a historical context. Walter Russell Mead and Eliot Cohen each argue in slightly different ways that there is a continuity in American grand strategy. Through analysis of their arguments, it is clear that US actions in Lebanon from 1982 to 1983, and Iraq in 2003 should be viewed not as isolated anomalies, but as part of a continuum in foreign-policy trends that have roots, which extend back to the founding of the nation.

Walter Russell Mead

In Mead's view, there are at least four distinguishable patterns in US Foreign Policy when viewed over long periods of time.[29] In the book, *Power, Terror, Peace, and War*, Mead categorizes these trends and those that advocate them as Economic Nationalists Hamiltonians, Idealistic Internationalists Wilsonians, Isolationist Jeffersonians, and Populist Nationalist Jacksonians.[30] Mead's central argument is that each of these schools of thought are ingrained in the American DNA and that at different times, based on a myriad of complex reasons, mostly tied to internal economic conditions and external threats, they vie for supremacy in domestic politics. The winner in those competitions for influence plays a predictable role in determining foreign policy and US grand strategy.[31]

Mead argues that since the 1920s the competition has mainly been between the Idealistic Internationalist Wilsonians, and the Populist Nationalist Jacksonians.[32] Mead contends that the Wilsonians see an inseparable link between US long-term security and the spread of American liberal values.[33] The interventionist tendencies of the Wilsonians are balanced by the Jacksonians, who fervently oppose big government, international organizations, and long-term US over-seas commitments to nation building.[34] In Mead's view, the Jacksonians are not isolationists, instead, they represent the hawks of foreign policy, quick to use military force to protect vital interests. Rather than seek security through the establishment of like values, Jacksonians seek security through the threat of overwhelming force.[35] This American preference for overwhelming firepower and direct violent assault was also recognized by Russell Weigley, in his seminal work *The American Way of War.*[36]

The thrust of Mead's argument is that most Americans have always supported the effort to build a safer, more economically stable world that values human rights.[37] The question is whether it is better to use global liberal institutions and governments or the threat and use of punitive force to achieve the objective. Because neither school of thought is able to completely control the development of foreign policy, "there will always be contradictions, tensions, and uneasy compromises," in US grand strategy.[38] These contradictions, tensions, and uneasy compromises will be highlighted in later case studies of Lebanon and Iraq in chapters 4 and 5.

Eliot Cohen

In 1973, when Cohen wrote *The Strategy of Innocence?*, his thesis was that US national security policy reflected and was still influenced by the period of 1920 to 1945.[39] Like Mead, Cohen believes the policy makers of the 1920s were heavily influenced by the legacy of President Woodrow Wilson, "American decision makers came to see in the experience of the depression and spread of militaristic and totalitarian regimes a confirmation of Wilson's basic view that a liberal world order was the only guarantee of American Safety."[40] Cohen also believed that the period brought about four primary trends in American Foreign Policy that have continued to persist. First, because of Pearl Harbor and the threat posed by the rise of the Soviet Union, policy makers demanded military readiness and the ability to prevent surprise attacks. This in turn led to the acceptance of a large peacetime military with a permanent presence. Because the threats were external, policy makers viewed national security on global rather than local terms. Finally, a trend we will see brought out again in case studies of Lebanon and Iraq, the military developed, "a persistent preference for excessively neat patterns of civil-military relations."[41]

In the *Strategy of Innocence?* Cohen also talks about what Mead termed the contradictions, tensions, and uneasy compromises in US grand strategy. The US, according to Cohen, was forced during World War II to make several difficult choices between short-term and long-term goals.[42] In 1940 and 1941, the US had to decide whether it was going to conserve its resources for the defense of the Western Hemisphere or deplete them in support of the defense of the United Kingdom.[43] Another example of uneasy compromise highlighted by Cohen is that although the US was leery of the long-term intentions of China and the Soviet Union, it was forced to provide the support needed to keep them in the war.[44] Thus, while the grand strategy may be simplistically described as doing what was required to achieve the goal of "unconditional surrender," it is clear that there were many competing interests and views on the appropriate way to accomplish that goal. As we will see in the later chapters, the debate about what to do and how, is a constant factor in development of grand strategy. This debate will play a prominent role in contributing to a dysfunctional relationship between the Department of Defense and the State Department in both Lebanon and Iraq.

The case studies of Lebanon and Iraq will also show that there is a tendency in US strategy to "Americanize" the solution by asking the military to use overwhelming force in ways that are clearly contrary to the political objectives. Cohen saw the same thing in World War II, saying that the conflict shaped and revealed two distinct characteristics of American strategic culture: "The preference for massing a vast array of men and machines and the predilection for direct and violent assault."[45]

Mead and Cohen both argue that in the formulation of grand strategy there will always be contradictions, tensions, and uneasy compromises. The presence of these conflicts can be attributed to the differences between the schools of thought that have evolved within US strategic planning circles. Both historians demonstrate that the dominant characteristics of American strategic culture can be revealed through examination of virtually every military engagement since 1920. One of the dominant characteristics is that the military's preference for excessively neat civil-military relations precludes diplomats and generals from working hand-in-hand to craft holistic, yet nuanced strategies. This lack of cooperation leads to conflict over what to do and how to do it. Finally, historical analysis shows that while sorting through these complexities and tensions, America's Jeffersonian preference for overwhelming firepower and direct violent assault takes the lead and often undermines the very goals the US is trying to achieve.

Again, the case studies in chapters 4 and 5 will show that with slight variations on Mead's and Cohen's themes, US actions in Lebanon and Iraq can be viewed as part of a continuum of American grand strategy with roots that date back to the founding of the nation.

Dennis Drew and Dr. Donald Snow

Perhaps the best definition of grand strategy can be found in a book entitled *Making Strategy: An Introduction to National Security Processes and Problems* by Dennis Drew and Donald Snow. For the authors, the role of strategy is to define and implement the means necessary to achieve national interests or ends.[46] The means are typically described in terms of instruments of power: diplomacy, information, military, and economy, while the ends are usually expressed in terms of national interests such as protecting the homeland or ensuring vital sea-lanes remain navigable.[47] Within this framework, Drew and Snow define Grand National Strategy as "the process by which the appropriate instruments of power are arrayed and employed to accomplish the national interests."[48] Thus, the two parts of grand strategy are the vital interests the nation is trying to achieve or protect and the instruments being used to achieve or protect those interests.[49]

Naturally, the question becomes how does a nation define vital interests? Drew and Snow contend that all vital interests have two components in common. First, the nation is "unwilling to compromise" on the interest and second, in addition to being unwilling to compromise, in order for an interest to be vital, the nation must be willing to employ military force to protect the interest.[50] In *America Overcommitted*, Donald Nuechterlein, presents a framework for determining which interests are worth fighting over and which are not.[51] Nuechterlein subdivides national interests into four distinct categories: Survival, Vital, Major, and Peripheral, as shown in the following chart.

Nuechterlein defines a survival interest as one that threatens the physical existence of a nation. Vital interests are those that can create serious harm if not met with strong measures, including application of military force. Major interests are those which may negatively impact the well-being of the nation, however, the use of military force is not deemed appropriate. Finally, Nuechterlein defines peripheral interests as being the least important and generally having little impact on the nation as a whole.[53] Survival interests and peripheral interests are fairly easy for a nation to categorize and there is usually little debate regarding the level of importance of the given interest. In contrast, the differentiation between vital and major interests is often contentious and requires considerable debate. The categorization of the interests in these two categories often shift back and forth between being considered vital or major depending on the views of the actors making the decision. These debates are especially contentious because the dividing line between the two represents which interests will be defended with force and which will not.[54] Once the vital interests have been determined, they must be matched with the means used to achieve or protect them.

As mentioned previously, the instruments of national power are the means used to achieve or protect national interests. Joint Publication 1, *Doctrine for the Armed Forces of the United States*, defines instruments of national power as the tools the US uses to apply its power. They include diplomacy, information, military force, and economic strength.[55] Diplomacy refers to the ways the diplomatic skills of the nation can be used to pursue national interests.[56] Joint doctrine states that, diplomacy is the tool used to engage with other states and foreign groups to advance the United States' values, interests, and objectives.[57] Information, according to Todd Kiefer, can best be thought of as awareness or a set of beliefs and perceived facts upon which decisions are made.[58] Information, as an instrument of national power, is used to influence domestic and foreign citizens, adversaries, and governments through the free exchange of ideas.[59] The military instrument is perhaps the easiest to understand in that the military is used, or its use is threatened, to achieve national interest through the application of violence by the armed forces. The final tool that can be used to achieve, or protect national interests, is the economy. The economic instrument of national power is often used to apply the carrot-and-stick approach to other nations. Economic aide and trade agreements are used as enticements to persuade other nations to help the US achieve or protect its national interests, while sanctions and tariffs are used to punish those who threaten US interests.[60] Ultimately, the role of the strategist is to determine what instruments of national power are, "available, appropriate, and acceptable" for use in achieving the national objectives.[61] Providing direction and coordinating the activities of the various departments within the US Government capable of applying the instruments of national power is the responsibility of the National Security Council.[62]

Conclusion

This chapter began with an examination of Clausewitz's definition of "policy" as the "trustee of all the interest of the state," the "great outlines" upon which war was planned and carried out.[63] Policy, in Clausewitz's work, unified and reconciled all the aspects of the internal administration.[64] Yet Clausewitz failed to acknowledge the complexity or friction involved in formulating a policy that could be used as a grand strategy. Liddell Hart expanded on Clausewitz to say that grand strategy was more than policy, it was policy in action. "The [coordination and direction] of all the resources of a nation…towards the attainment of the political object of the war—the goal defined by the fundamental policy."[65] Liddell Hart addressed the complexity Clausewitz chose to ignore, by describing how grand strategy must go beyond military force and incorporate financial pressure, diplomatic pressure, and ethical pressure in a holistic manner.

Upon this theoretical foundation, the works of Mead and Cohen were used to demonstrate the historical context in which Lebanon and Iraq fit in the continuum of US grand strategy. The authors highlighted the contradictions, tensions, and uneasy compromises that must be made when grand strategy moves from theory to practice.

Finally, Drew and Snow were used to show that there are two components to grand strategy: the vital interests the nation is trying to achieve or protect, and the instruments being used to achieve or protect those interests. The next chapter will focus on the structure of the US Government and how in theory, grand strategy is formulated and implemented within that structure.

Notes

1. B. H. Liddell Hart, *Strategy*, 2nd ed. (London: Meridian Printing, 1991), 322.

2. Antulio Echevaria, *Clausewitz and Contemporary War* (New York: Oxford University Press, 2007), 14-16. Echevaria believes Clausewitz used Immanuel Kant's system of logic; however, he did it indirectly, through the lectures and textbooks of Johann Kiesewetter, who taught at the General War School in Berlin.

3. Eschevaria.

4. Howard and Paret, *On War*, 89.

5. It is in this note of 1827 that Clausewitz asserts "war is a continuation of state policy." Hew Strachan, *Clausewitz's On War: A Biography* (New York: Atlantic Monthly Press, 2007), 77.

6. Beatrice Heuser, Introduction to the abridged edition of *On War*, by Michael Howard and Peter Paret, eds., *On War* (Princeton, NJ: Princeton University Press, 1984).

7. Heuser.

8. Heuser.

9. Howard and Paret, *On War*, 227.

10. Strachan, *Clausewitz's On War*, 73.

11. Heuser, Introduction to *On War*.

12. Strachan, *Clausewitz's On War*, 26-27.

13. Strachan, 78.

14. CB20120327G0001, Senior British Official, Interview by Charles Bris-Bois, 27 March 2012, United Kingdom.

15. CB20120327G0001, Senior British Official.

16. Howard and Paret, *On War*, 609-610.

17. CB20120327G0001, Senior British Official, Interview by Charles Bris-Bois.

18. Howard and Paret, *On War*, 606-610.

19. Howard and Paret, 606.

20. Howard and Paret, 607.

21. Echevaria, *Clausewitz and Contemporary War*, Chapter 4.

22. Echevaria.

23. Liddell Hart, *Strategy*, Introduction.

24. Hart, 353.

25. Hart, 343.

26. Hart, 322.

27. Hart.

28. Hart.

29. Walter Russell Mead, *Power, Terror, Peace, and War* (New York: Knopf, 2004), 19.

30. Walter Russell Mead, *Special Providence* (New York: Knopf, 2001).

31. Mead makes this argument in both *Power, Terror, Peace; and War,* and *Special Providence.*

32. Mead, Chapters 5 and 6.

33. Mead, *Special Providence,* Chapter 2. Mead believes that the Wilsonian school has its active interventionist roots in the missionaries and fervent Protestants that first settled America. For Mead, Wilsonian liberal values can be interpreted as opposition to militaristic and totalitarian regimes, but the original Wilsonians did not believe the spread of democratic society was practical in many parts of the world.

34. Mead, *Power, Terror, Peace, and War*, 98.

35. Mead, *Special Providence.* 218.

36. Russell Weigley, *The American Way of War* (Bloomington: Indiana University Press 1977.)

37. Mead, *Power, Terror, Peace, and War*, 7.

38. Mead.

39. Eliot Cohen, "The Strategy of Innocence? The United States, 1920-1945," in *The Making of Strategy: Rules, States, and War,* eds. Williamson Murray, MacGregor Knox, and Alvin Bernstein (New York: Cambridge University Press, 1994), 428-465.

40. Cohen, 454.

41. Cohen, 453.

42. Cohen, 455.

43. Cohen.

44. The US counted on the Soviets to wear down the Germans through attrition in the European theater, and in China expected to use ports and airfields along the east coast to launch attacks on the Japanese main islands. Cohen, *The Strategy of Innocence?*, 455.

45. Cohen, "The Strategy of Innocence?" 464.

46. Col Dennis M. Drew and Dr. Donald M. Snow, *Making Strategy: An Introduction to National Security Processes and Problems* (Maxwell, AL: Air University Press, 1988), 27.

47. Drew and Snow; When Drew and Snow wrote *Making Strategy* in 1988, the instruments of national power did not include information. Drew and Snow list the instruments as simply, political/diplomatic, economic and military. Current Joint Doctrine as seen in JP-1, 2009 uses the newer definition to define instruments of national power as Diplomatic, Informational, Military and Economic (DIME).

48. Drew and Snow.

49. Drew and Snow.

50. Drew and Snow, 28.

51. Donald Nuechterlein, *America Overcommitted: United States National Interests in the 1980s* (Lexington: University of Kentucky Press, 1985).

52. Donald Nuechterlein.

53. Donald Nuechterlein.

54. Drew and Snow, *Making Strategy*, 30.

55. Joint Chiefs of Staff, Joint Publication (JP) 1, *Doctrine for the Armed Forces of the United States* (Washington, DC: Government Printing Office, 2007, Incorporating Change 1, 20 March 2009), I-8.

56. Drew and Snow, *Making Strategy,* 36.

57. Joint Chiefs of Staff, JP 1, I-9.

58. Todd Kiefer, "Competition, War and Transformation: Interagency Framework for Operational Planning and Force Development" (Briefing on 2 June 2004), www.au.af mil/au/awc/awcgate/jcs/competition.ppt/ (accessed 1 March 2012). At the time of the briefing in 2004, Todd Kiefer was a Commander in the United States Navy working on the Joint Staff J7 at the Pentagon.

59. Joint Chiefs of Staff, JP 1, 1-9.

60. Drew and Snow, *Making Strategy,* 37.

61. Drew and Snow, 43.

62. Joint Chiefs of Staff, JP 1, I-8.

63. Howard and Paret, *On War,* 606-610.

64. Howard and Paret, 606.

65. Liddell Hart, *Strategy,* 322.

Chapter 3
How The Government Creates
Grand Strategy

The Executive Branch has far more often than not failed to formulate, in an integrated and coherent manner judiciously using resources drawn from all elements of national power, a mid-and long-term strategy necessary to defend and further those interests vital to the nation's security.[1]
—Don M. Snider, *The National Security Strategy:*
Documenting Strategic Vision

Grand strategy was defined by Liddell Hart in the last chapter as the coordination and direction of all the resources of a nation toward achieving the political objective.[2] Snow and Drew expressed a similar belief in the meaning of grand strategy by defining it as, the coordination and direction of all the resources of a nation towards the achievement of political objectives.[3] Having established these definitions, the question becomes: How does the US government create and implement an agreed upon grand strategy? This chapter will explain why grand strategy development and implementation is not an easy thing for a democratic government that divides power between the executive and legislative branches. In theory, the National Security Council has evolved to overcome these difficulties through an interagency process that brings the whole-of-government together to advise the president and help determine what the grand strategy should be and which Cabinets within the government should be responsible for its implementation. This chapter will begin with a short historical examination of past United States grand strategies, followed by an introduction to the National Security Council. Within the National Security Council, the role of Presidential Decision Documents will be used to illuminate how policy is created, and how that policy then through action, becomes grand strategy.

History of United States Grand Strategy

World War II

Historians and political scientists generally agree that the best example of the US creating and implementing a coherent and coordinated grand strategy occurred at the onset of World War II. Recognizing that the US could potentially be drawn into a two-theater conflict, one in Europe and one in the Pacific, President Franklin Roosevelt and his administration, decided even before the attack on Pearl Harbor, that if the US had to fight both Germany and Japan, that the majority of the resources and focus would be directed toward Europe.[4] After the defeat of the Nazis, the US would then turn its attention toward the Pacific. In reality, the US expended considerable resources and focus on the Pacific Theater prior to the defeat of Germany, yet Roosevelt's Europe-First Policy and its subsequent implementation, are held up as the model of grand strategy, because all decisions regarding the application of the instruments of national power were made with this policy as the fundamental starting point.[5]

Although scholars hold up the vignette of Word War II as the classic example of grand strategy, the politicians of the time found great fault in the manner in which the US mobilized and fought the war. Specifically, in 1947 the Senate Armed Services Committee, found that it took far too long to mobilize the armed forces, resources were used in a wasteful manner, intelligence on enemy capabilities and intentions was lacking, and most significantly, there was a disconnect between military objectives and political purpose.[6] A similar report from the House of Representatives laid out the roadmap for what would eventually be adopted as the National Security Act of 1947. Recognizing the next war may not afford the US time to mobilize and deploy forces the way it had for World War I and World War II, the report called for a complete overhaul of the nation's national security architecture. Among the recommendations were several new organizations; Department of Defense, Joint Chiefs of Staff, Office of the Secretary of Defense, and the National Security Council.[7] The purpose of these new entities was to ensure that all policy decisions, whether they be domestic, foreign or purely military in nature, were formed with the best information available from across the government. The hope was that with the ability to more efficiently tap into the nation's industry, manpower, and academia the government would be better stewards of available resources, and would position the US to be better prepared for the next war.[8]

Cold War (1945 to 1988)

While the National Security Act of 1947 was focused on ensuring the US was prepared for the next big war, the administration of Harry S. Truman worked vigorously to draft and implement a new grand strategy that would minimize the chance of a Third World War, and at the same time stop Soviet sponsored communist expansion around the globe. "Relying on the experience of the 1930s interwar years as their frame of reference, they were convinced that appeasement of totalitarian states during that period had encouraged Axis aggression. [The Truman Administration] therefore adopted the position that Communist Russia represented an ominous threat the United States had to resist."[9] As a result, Containment became the grand strategy of the US Similar to the Europe-First Policy, the policy of Containment gave the government a conceptual framework upon which to base all decisions on how to align and execute all the instruments of national power. Historians largely agree that this grand strategy worked well for over four decades, lasting from its implementation in 1947 up until the collapse of the Soviet Union, 1987 to 1991.[10]

Post Cold War (1988 to 2001)

Following the collapse of the Soviet Union, with Containment no longer necessary, President Clinton had to create a new grand strategy. Later in his presidency, when asked by a Cable News Network reporter whether or not there was a "Clinton-Doctrine," President Clinton responded by saying he believed it was, "bringing the world together to stop genocide and ethnic cleansing."[11] Although that may be how the President would like to be remembered, the reality is that the Clinton Administration's grand strategy was creating policies and aligning the instruments of national power to, "batter down barriers to United States' trade and investment."[12] There was a fundamental belief in both George H.W. Bush's and Clinton's administrations that the opening of world markets to United States' goods would not only benefit the US in economic terms, but it would lead to a more peaceful world. As many prominent political scientists pointed out at the time; no two nations with McDonald's hamburger restaurants had ever gone to war with each other.[13] Thus, the implementation of the North American Free Trade Act and the World Trade Organization, moved to the top of the Clinton Administration's priority list. President Clinton championed the principle of engagement as the preferred method of dealing with both allies and competitors. But because the US no longer had a competitor which could credibly muster enough power to balance or counter-act the United States' desires, the US was essentially able to dictate to the rest of the world how it would act in foreign affairs. A prime example of this being Europe's inability to change President Clinton's approach to dealing with Bosnia and Kosovo.[14] Because Africa and South Asia did not fit into this grand strategy of economic expansion, the US largely ignored these regions and their problems, as evidenced by the closing of a large number of embassies and consulates in areas not seen as vital in advancing the United States' vital interests.[15] Many believe that the combination of the collapse of the super-power dominated world order, and America's subsequent withdrawal from regions deemed unimportant, allowed al-Qaeda the ability to expand and exploit areas in South Asia and Africa left behind by globalization.

Post 9/11

Following the tragic attacks on the World Trade Center and the Pentagon by al-Qaeda on 11 September 2001, President George W. Bush moved away from Clinton's principle of engagement in international relations and moved toward a unilateralist approach that warned both friends and enemies, "Every nation, in every region, now has a decision to make. Either you are with us, or you are with the terrorists."[16] Bush's grand strategy was now singularly focused on doing whatever was required to prevent another attack on the US homeland. The foundation of this defense of the homeland was an offensive military campaign aimed at destroying terrorist groups that threatened the US and her allies around the world.[17] To gain this security for the homeland and help in destroying terrorist networks, the Bush Administration was willing to completely alter the nature of the relationships it had with other nations and governments. The Taliban, once heavily courted as partner in building an oil pipeline that would divert Caspian Sea oil through Afghanistan to Pakistani ports under the Clinton and Bush Administrations, was now "Enemy #1" due to their refusal to hand over Osama bin Laden.[18] Pakistan, which previously had fallen out of favor with the US because of their Nuclear Weapons programs, went from being a target of sanctions, to the United States' "most important military partner."[19] Russia, originally deemed by the Bush Administration to be "weak and irrelevant" became an increasingly important partner due to their experience fighting the Islamic extremist in Chechnya. Finally, Africa went from being a continent that held very few vital interests for the US, to a continent that had to be engaged to ensure that al-Qaeda did not leave Afghanistan, only to reform in another ungoverned space within Africa.[20] The key concept to understand, as highlighted by these examples, is that the Bush Administration changed the definition of United States' National Interests after September 11th. As discussed above, the previous definition of national interests under the Clinton Administration was anything that helped expand trade and investment. After September 11th, national interests, "revolved completely around internal debates over what was required for the nation's security."[21] As we'll see in the next section, those internal debates, in theory, are supposed to take place within the National Security Council.

The National Security Council

The National Security Council was created as part of the larger National Security Act of 1947. Prior to World War II, the US Government dealt with complex problems as individual departments—the State Department, the War Department, the Department of the Navy, and the Treasury—with the help and guidance of the president. As the US emerged from World War II, with an unprecedented global leadership role, it recognized that the stove-piped approach to dealing with international affairs no longer worked. Instead global leadership required a combination of diplomacy, economic enticement, and military strength.[22] The National Security Council was created as a means of bringing together the disparate departments under the Executive Branch in order to "mitigate the problems that [arose] from the way the United States Government is structured."[23] The National Security Act of 1947 did not knock down the stove-pipes, but "it did bend them at the top so that the policy thoughts coming from each would come together [within the National Security Council]."[24]

Per Section 101 of Title I. of the National Security Act entitled, Coordination for National Security, the purpose of the National Security Council is threefold. The first objective of the National Security Council is to advise the president on how best to integrate foreign, domestic, and military policies of the US to achieve national security objectives. The second purpose of the National Security Council is to assess and appraise the objectives, commitments, and risks associated with the United States' National Security Policy. The final purpose of the National Security Council as laid out in the National Security Act is to review and consider all national security policies that have common interests across the departments and agencies of the government.[25] The purpose of the National Security Council is to ensure the president regularly looks at all the facets of "complex multidimensional issues" and provides guidance that can then be carried out in a coordinated fashion by the various departments and agencies.[26]

The National Security Advisor is the person responsible for ensuring the president receives multiple points of view from all departments and agencies involved in a given policy debate. Due to the way the National Security Advisor was created under the Dwight Eisenhower Administration, there is no congressional mandate for the position or formal guidance on the duties and responsibilities of the National Security Advisor.[27] According to Donald Rumsfeld, successful National Security Advisors perform three key roles. First, they identify where policy guidance from the president is necessary. Then they manage the interagency debate to ensure the president receives the information needed to make informed decisions and provide guidance to the administration. Finally, the National Security Advisor should ensure that the president's decisions are understood by all and carried out in the manner prescribed.[28] The National Security Advisor does this by working with the President and the interagency staff to formulate and issue Presidential Decision Directives.

Presidential Decision Directives

Presidential Decision Directives are designed to create intensive interaction among the agencies of the US Government. The process begins when the President, normally through the National Security Advisor, issues a Presidential Review Directive, "which tasks the relevant agencies to develop a new policy based on broad guidance."[29] In order to be effective, the Presidential Decision Directive has to bring together all of the relevant agencies from within the whole-of-government. When President Clinton wanted to formulate his Latin American Policy, he sent his Presidential Review Directive to 21 separate agencies within the government, thus bringing together both those agencies with direct ties to Latin America and those agencies whose policies had second and third order effects on Latin America.[30] In theory, once each agency receives the Presidential Review Directive, with the President's broad guidance, they assign an office or person within their particular agency to represent their organization's interests in the larger interagency debate that will result in a Presidential Decision Directive. Once the Presidential Decision Directive is issued, the heads of the agencies are then tasked to ensure that their agency's policies and actions align with the new Presidential Decision Directive. Often, these shifts require resources, which must be added to the agency or taken from another program. Because Congress holds the purse strings, the changes must be "costed out and submitted....for approval and funding, without which policy is merely words of hopeful expectations."[31] Grand strategy truly begins after the interagency debates have been settled, the President has issued a Presidential Decision Directive, the applicable agencies of the government have determined what adjustments are needed to meet the intent of the Presidential Decision Directive and Congress has provided the funding and approval to make the necessary changes. One relatively recent Presidential Decision Directive stands out due to the fact that it outlined how to more effectively use the interagency process.

Presidential Decision Directive 56: The Clinton Administration's Policy on Managing Complex Contingency Operations

In 1996, President Clinton's National Security Staff looked back at the way the interagency handled complex contingency operations in Panama (1989 to 1990), Somalia (1992 to 1994), and Haiti (1994 to 1995). Because there were no set guidelines on how each of these contingency operations should be handled, they were all approached and conducted in a somewhat ad-hoc manner.[33] Presidential Directive 56 attempted to take the best interagency lessons from these events and institutionalize them so that the US and the interagency in particular, would be better prepared to handle them.[34] "The philosophy behind the document is that interagency planning can make or break a [military] operation."[35] The Directive tried to effect change in the interagency process by recommending five broad reforms: creation of an Executive Committee, the requirement for a detailed political-military implementation plan, interagency rehearsals, interagency after-action reviews, and training for policy makers on how to effectively use the interagency process.[36] After Presidential Directive 56 was published, the Clinton administration attempted to apply its principles in several contingency operations including Kosovo (1998 to 1999). The after-action report from Kosovo highlighted the "recurring problems of the interagency: the need for decisive authority (nobody's in charge), contrasting approaches and institutional cultures (particularly diplomatic versus military) with respect to planning, and the lack of incentives across the government to create professionals expert in interagency work."[37] Thus, while Presidential Directive 56 attempted to take the best practices from previous experiences and institutionalize them, it could not overcome the inherent faults that are built into the interagency system: lack of authority, cultural differences, and lack of incentives to put the interagency success above individual agency parochialism.

The Reality of Grand Strategy

The reality of strategic policy making is that grand strategy is not always well thought through and staffed through the interagency process of Presidential Review Directives, interagency debate, and Presidential Decision Directives. Often times, administrations find that "speeches, press conferences, VIP visits, and presidential travel" contribute to the development of policy as much as the formal interagency process.[38] The United States' push for NATO expansion is a prime example of policy formulation outside the normal National Security Council process, and is a cautionary tale of what can be missed when policies are formed without regard to grand strategy. In September of 1994, as the Clinton Administration pushed a proposal to expand NATO membership to include the Czech Republic, Poland, and Hungary; members of the NATO briefing team visited Yale University to sell their proposal. During the question and answer session that followed, Professor Bruce Russett stood and asked several pointed questions such as: Could this proposal undermine President Yeltsin's efforts to democratize Russia? Could this drive Russia into some type of alliance with China? "Then one of the briefers exclaimed, in front of [the] entire audience:—Good God!—We'd never thought of that!"[39] The genesis of the NATO expansion came from a brief meeting in the Oval Office between Polish President Lech Walesa, Czech President Vaclav Havel, and President Clinton. When the two Eastern European leaders asked President Clinton to include the Czech Republic, Poland, and Hungary in NATO, he agreed on the spot and from that day forward began using speeches, press conferences, and presidential travel to extol NATO expansion.[40]

The interagency process was created to ensure that the second and third order effects of policy decisions were thought of, and that the whole-of-government was brought together to offer the President the best advice on how to proceed based on policies and stated grand strategies. As this example clearly shows, the interagency process is not always used effectively or as it was intended. The remainder of this paper will endeavor to explain how the interagency was used to develop a grand strategy for Lebanon in 1982 and Iraq in 2003.

Notes

1. Don M. Snider and John A. Nagl, *The National Security Strategy: Documenting Strategic Vision* (Carlisle, PA: US Army War College, 2001).

2. Liddell Hart, *Strategy*, 322.

3. Drew and Snow, *Making Strategy,* 27.

4. Daniel W. Drezner, "Values, Interests, and American Grand Strategy," danieldrezner.com/research/leffler.pdf (accessed 7 April 2012).

5. For more information on President Roosevelt and World War II see: Eric Larrabee, *Commander in Chief: Franklin Delano Roosevelt;* and Waldo Heinrich, *Franklin D. Roosevelt and the American Entry into WWII.*

6. Gregory D. Foster, McNair Paper 27, *In Search of Post-Cold War Security Structure* (Washington, DC: National Defense University, Institute for National Strategic Studies, February 1994).

7. Foster, 10.

8. Foster.

9. Foster.

10. Drezner, 430.

11. Walter Lafeber, "The Bush Doctrine," *Diplomatic History* 26, no. 4 (2002): 543-558.

12. Lafeber, 543.

13. Thomas Friedman first presented this theory in his book *"The Lexus and the Olive Tree."* The theory was disproven when Russia and Georgia went to war. Both nations had McDonalds in 2008 when the war occurred.

14. Lafeber, "Bush Doctrine," 549.

15. Lafeber, 544.

16. President George W. Bush, "Address to a Joint Session of Congress and the American People," 20 September 2001, georgewbush-whitehouse.archives.gov/news/releases/2001/09/20010920-8 html (accessed 15 April 2012).

17. Lafeber, "Bush Doctrine," 549.

18. Lafeber, "Bush Doctrine," 546. The negotiations to build the pipeline with the Taliban originally fell apart under the Clinton administration, due to US concerns over Taliban human rights abuses and the treatment of women. The Bush Administration tried to restart the negotiations but was hampered by the fact that Bin Laden was now residing in the country and he had been blamed for the US Embassy bombings in Kenya and Tanzania and the attack on the USS Cole.

19. Lafeber, "Bush Doctrine," 548.

20. Lafeber.

21. Lafeber.

22. Donald Rumsfeld, *Known and Unknown: A Memoir* (New York, Sentinel, 2011), 317.

23. Rumsfeld.

24. Rumsfeld.

25. Richard A. Best, *The National Security Council: An Organizational Assessment* (Washington, DC: Congressional Research Service, 2009).

26. Rumsfeld, *Known and Unknown,* 318.

27. Best, *The National Security Council,* 8.

28. Rumsfeld, *Known and Unknown,* 324.

29. Gabriel Marcella, "National Security and the Interagency Process: Forward into the 21st Century," in *US Army War College Guide to Strategy,* eds. Joseph R. Cerami, James F. Holcomb, and Army War College (Carlisle Barracks, PA: Strategic Studies Institute, US Army War College, 2001).

30. Marcella, 117.

31. Marcella.

32. When President George W. Bush was elected President, one of the first things he did was change the nomenclature from Presidential Decision Directives (PDDs) to National Security Presidential Directives (NSPD). For an excellent analysis of the National Security Council. See: Gabriel Marcella, *Affairs of State: The Interagency and National Security* (Washington, DC: National Strategic Studies Institute, December 2008), StrategicStudiesInstitute.army.mil/pdffiles/Pub896.pdf (accessed 15 March 2012).

33. John T. Fishel, *Civil-Military Operations in the New World* (New York: Praeger, 1997).

34. Marcella, *Affairs of State,* 118.

35. Marcella.

36. Fishel, *Civil-Military Operations,* 95.

37. Marcella, *Affairs of State,* 119.

38. Marcella, 112.

39. John L. Gaddis, *What is Grand Strategy* (Duke University, Keynote address for a conference on "American Grand Strategy after War," 2009).

40. Gaddis, 4. For a complete description of how NATO expansion became US policy, see: James M. Goldgeier, *Not Whether but When: the US Decision to Enlarge NATO* (Washington, DC: Brookings Institution Press, 1999).

Chapter 4
Lebanon Case Study

Instead of promoting a rapprochement between Israel and its neighbors, the application of US force and diplomacy had succeeded only in pushing these objectives beyond all reach.[1]
—Ralph A. Hallenbeck, *Military Force as an Instrument of US Foreign Policy*

Understanding how the United States Became Involved

The United States' initial history of involvement in Lebanon began in May of 1958, when then Lebanese President Camille Chamoun asked President Eisenhower to deploy US forces to Lebanon in order to dissuade Syria from invading. Although reluctant, Eisenhower agreed to employ US forces based on three factors. First, Eisenhower was alarmed by the increasing Soviet influence in Syria. Second, Eisenhower believed the US had to support allies who stood against the Pan-Arabism that was sweeping the region. Finally, the pro-American government in Iraq had just been overthrown and executed, leading the US to fear that the government in Lebanon would be next if support was not given.[2] Therefore, Eisenhower agreed to send 5,000 Marines and a contingent of US Army soldiers to Lebanon for six months.[3] The first US intervention in Lebanon ended when it became clear that the Syrians no longer intended to invade and the situation stabilized. According to a Central Intelligence Agency analyst, who was stationed at the US Embassy in Lebanon in 1982 and interviewed as part of this research, the presence of US forces was credited with providing time needed for the rival Lebanese factions to agree on the election of a new President, which in-turn led to a semblance of political stability and a lack of outright hostility between the factions for nearly 20 years. That peace held until the outbreak of the 1975 civil war.[4]

Lebanese Civil War

The origins of the 1975 Lebanese Civil War cannot be separated from the larger issues of the Middle East, namely the enduring conflict between the Israelis and the Palestinians. Following the 1973 Yom Kippur War, the US brokered the Camp David Peace Accords in which Egypt officially agreed to recognize Israel in return for Israel returning the Sinai to Egypt.[5] As part of the Camp David Peace Talks, Lebanon became a key area of foreign-policy interest to the US Following the precedent set by the Egyptians, the US attempted to get the Palestinians to recognize Israel's right to exist in return for Palestinian self-government in the occupied territories.

31

One of the major obstructions to the negotiations was the PLO, which because of its militancy, had already been "forcibly expelled" from Jordan and Syria, which did not want the PLO causing trouble within their borders. Unfortunately, Lebanon did not have a strong central government or strong military to prevent the PLO from taking refuge in southern Lebanon, where they prospered among the Palestinian refugee camps.[6] By 1975, there were 350,000 Palestinians in Lebanon.[7] This added to the already volatile balance of power between the Maronite Christians, the Lebanese Shia Muslims, and Druze within Lebanon.

In 1975, that strain exploded into a full civil war. Unable to control the factions, the Lebanese Army broke apart, forcing Lebanese President Suleiman Frangieh to ask Syria to intervene and stop the fighting, that was now almost completely along sectarian lines. The Syrians deployed 30,000 troops to Lebanon and from 1976 until 1982; they were able to quell the violence as "invited peacekeepers."[8] Despite the Syrian presence, all of the factions, "maintained well-armed militias, and [sought] outside support in order to ensure survival in the internecine Lebanese political environment."[9] In the run-up to the 1982 elections, the Phalange, the largest of the Maronite Christian factions, began vehemently voicing opposition to the presence of both the PLO and the Syrian peacekeepers in Lebanon. The Israelis recognized a natural partner in the Phalange and their Lebanese Forces Christian militia, because they were non-Muslim, anti-PLO, and anti-Syria.[10] To enhance this tie, the Israelis provided over $100 million to the Lebanese Forces Christian Militia between 1976 and 1982.[11] In return for this support, the Israelis expected and encouraged the Phalange to act as their proxy in attacking the PLO and Syria.[12]

When the PLO attempted to assassinate the Israeli Ambassador to the United Kingdom in early June 1982, the Israelis decided they could no longer accept the terrorist organization's presence on its border. They responded by launching "Operation Peace for Galilee" under the pretext that it would create a 25 mile cordon free of the PLO, pushing them beyond the range of their limited artillery and rockets.[13] However, within four days, Israeli troops had surpassed the 25 mile cordon and were at the outskirts of Beirut, where the PLO had retreated, and had dug in for a final fight.[14] The ensuing siege lasted from mid-June until 15 August 1982, when the Israelis accepted a United States-brokered deal to allow the PLO to peacefully leave Beirut, and resettle in eight separate Arab countries, (Jordan, Iraq, Tunisia, North Yemen, South Yemen, Syria, Sudan, and Algeria).[15]

Having few other options, the PLO agreed to this arrangement only after the US and Israel guaranteed safe passage of the fighters and protection of their families remaining in West Beirut from attack by the Phalange.[16] This guarantee would be backed by a Multi-National Force, which included 800 United States Marines, the French, and the Italians.[17]

Thus began the second US intervention into Lebanon, modeled on the 1958 intervention.[18] On August 25, 1982, Col James Mead and his 800 Marines joined 800 French and 400 Italian soldiers as part of the Multi-National Force charged with the safe evacuation of the PLO from Lebanon. By the first of September, the mission was complete and the Secretary of Defense, Caspar Weinberger, ordered the Marines to return to their ships and sail to Naples.[19] The reprieve was short-lived and on September 23, 1982 the Marines of the 32nd MAU were ordered to leave Naples and return to Beirut following the death of President-elect Bashir Gemayel, which will be covered in detail later in this chapter.

Following the assassination of Bashir Gemayel, the Lebanese National Assembly quickly moved to elect Amin Gemayel to replace his brother.[20] One of Gemayel's first official duties was requesting the return of the Multi-National Force, to ensure civil war did not rip the nation apart.[21] As the Italians, French, and Americans returned to Beirut, it was determined that the US would occupy the International Airport. Col Mead, the commander of the 32nd MAU, wanted to occupy the Old Sidon Road and high ground around the airport. However, he was not allowed to due to the fact that Israeli forces needed that particular route to move logistics to their dispersed forces. If the Americans allowed the Israelis to transit supplies through areas they controlled, it was feared they would be perceived as supporting the Israeli aggression.[22] This left the Marines in a vulnerable position of not controlling the roads around the airport or the high ground that overlooked the airport. For eight months, as the 22nd and 24th MAUs exchanged rotations in Lebanon, the Marines faced minor confrontations with the Syrians, the Lebanese Muslims, and the Israelis.[23] The US forces tried in vain to remain neutral, but the Multi-National Force as a whole became associated with the Phalange-dominated Lebanese government and as a result began to suffer more and more attacks from the Muslim opposition, which at this point was being heavily supported by Syria and to a lesser extent Iran.[24] These attacks steadily rose leading up to April 18, 1983, when the US Embassy in West Beirut was attacked by a suicide truck-bomb.[25]

The Israelis were also feeling the effects of the increased attacks by the Syrians and factions opposed to the Gemayel government. In September of 1983, they retreated from the Shouf Mountains to more defensible positions south of the Alawi River.[26] Because the Lebanese Army was still weak, it did not have the ability to fill the positions left by the Isrealis.[27] This allowed the Druze factions supported by Syria to contest sections of key terrain that overlooked the international airport. Recognizing the danger posed by allowing this area to fall into the hands of the anti-government forces, the US began using its naval gunfire in direct support of the Lebanese Armed Forces that were attempting to fill the vacated Israeli positions.[28] At first, the US used only five-inch guns from the *USS Bowen* and *USS John Rodgers* but then on September 25, 1983, the US shelled the Shouf mountains with the sixteen-inch guns of the *USS New Jersey.*[29] As the analysis later in this chapter will clearly show, this direct support of the Lebanese Armed Forces removed any pretext of neutrality and linked the Americans directly with the Phalange-dominated Gemayel government.[30]

Now clearly seen as the enemy, the Marines faced ever-increasing attacks and each time they responded in self-defense, they further eroded their status as peacekeepers. According to the Marine Commander at the time, Col Tim Geraghty, "The Muslim militias, Syrians, and the Iranians knew how to play this game. They created circumstances that quickly dissolved our purpose–a peacekeeping force–and then used our self-defense responses to rally and fan the flames of discontent among Muslim factions."[31] The flames of discontent culminated on October 23, 1983, when the Iranian Leftist group Islamic Amal, drove a nineteen-ton truck, loaded with twenty thousand pounds of TNT, into the Marine headquarters killing 241 Americans.[32]

The remainder of this chapter will demonstrate that while the initial reason for returning to Lebanon, the evacuation of the PLO, was tactically successful, a lack of a grand strategy led to decisions that fundamentally crippled the US mission in Lebanon and the larger peace process.

Why the United States' Mission in Lebanon Failed

The following case study on the United States' intervention into Lebanon in 1982 will show that the US failed to employ a grand strategy for five distinct reasons. First, there was a failure to recognize that ultimate success rested almost entirely on political reconciliation between the opposing factions within the Lebanese government, the PLO, and the Syrian government. Second, a lack of recognition of how US actions would affect political reconciliation led directly to a lack of consensus about what needed to be done and how to do it. Third, these disagreements erupted into personality disputes between Secretary of Defense Weinberger and Secretary of State Shultz, which in turn polarized the National Security Council and paralyzed it from fulfilling its assigned responsibilities. Fourth, when the Lebanese proved incapable or unwilling to solve their own problems, there was intense pressure from Washington to "Americanize" the solution. Finally, there was a lack of congruency between roles the military was given, objectives it was asked to achieve, and overarching United Foreign Policy objectives of the US.[33]

Military Mission Wholly Dependent on Political Reconciliation

If one were designing a grand strategy for the successful achievement of US interests in Lebanon, the first and most obvious requirement would be for political reconciliation between the factional groups, (Maronite Christians, Sunni Muslims, Palestinians, Shiite Muslims, and Druze,) all vying for a greater share of power. To an extent, the US recognized this early in 1982, prior to the second intervention.[34] The Reagan Administration was already engaged in the larger Arab-Israeli peace process in which it hoped to demonstrate that the US could act in an even-handed manner, seeking the best possible outcome for both the Arabs and the Israelis. By acting neutral, the US hoped that achieving progress on the larger Arab-Israeli problem would lead to political reconciliation within Lebanon. The process of political reconciliation and the desire to be viewed as a non-partisan player in the peace process failed, largely because the US failed to re-examine its strategic approach after two key events: the massacres at Sabra and Shatila, and the 17 May unilateral Israeli-Lebanon Agreement.

Sabra and Shatila

As discussed above, the evacuation of the PLO from Lebanon was a tactical success for the Multi National Force. With the PLO out of the country, the Lebanese Parliament met to elect a new President. Heavily supported both logistically and economically by the Israelis, the Phalange Maronite Christian candidate, Bashir Gemayel, easily won the election. The US, convinced that Lebanon was now on solid footing, removed the Marine contingent.[35] However, a suicide bomb attack killed Gemayel before he could officially assume the presidency. The Israelis, who had agreed not to enter the Muslim area of Western Beirut, as part of the PLO evacuation agreement, immediately broke the conditions of the cease-fire.[36] They moved on Western Beirut under the pretext that they were going to clear out any remaining PLO fighters. The reality was that only the elderly, women, and small children remained in the camp. As the Israelis surrounded Sabra and Shatila, the Phalange Christians entered the camp and massacred thousands of women and children as retribution for the killing of Gemayel.[37] World sentiment quickly turned against the Israelis, who had the ability to stop the attack but chose not to, and the Americans who had prematurely departed Lebanon even though they had guaranteed the safety of the remaining Palestinians as part of the cease-fire agreement.[38] Under intense international pressure, President Reagan agreed to send the Marines back into Beirut, thus beginning the third US intervention in Lebanon.

This event marked the first instance where the US should have re-examined its grand strategy to determine what political and military adjustments needed to be made to ensure United States' objectives in Lebanon were achieved. The questions that should have been answered are: Is there a realistic chance for political reconciliation between the factions after the massacres, or are the ruling Maronite Christians going to have to force the other factions into submission? If Gemayel is going to have to subdue the rival factions, are the Lebanese Armed Forces (LAF) capable of doing so, without splintering along sectarian lines? Should the US Marines train the LAF? Is it wise for the US to be perceived as the backer of the Maronite Christians who are subduing Muslim factions, and how will such a perception affect the greater Middle East peace process? If the US chooses to back Geyamel's government, is it willing to use military force to ensure the Israelis and Syrians do not interfere in Lebanese internal politics?

The answers to these questions would have formed the basis of grand strategy and helped both the State Department and the Department of Defense craft operational strategies to achieve the desired results. Unfortunately, because there was little time and the US was under intense pressure to respond, the Marines were sent in with the vague mission of providing presence.

This event also marks the beginning of the irreconcilable split between the Department of State and the Department of Defense within the Reagan Administration. For Casper Weinberger, the Secretary of Defense, the massacre at Sabra and Shatila was a clear example of factional fighting and which the US should not become entangled in.[39] Already angered that the US had been drawn into the Lebanese conflict by what he viewed as Israel's illegitimate siege of Beirut, he believed that the US should virtually cut all ties with Israel.[40] Certainly, if the US wanted to retain the position of an honest broker to the Arab people, the US should have strongly condemned the Israeli Government and demanded concessions in the peace process, but the US did neither.

17 May Agreement

As the fighting continued throughout the remainder of 1982 and into early 1983, the US could do very little to convince the Israelis and Syrians to withdraw from Lebanon. Israel demanded that the US provide more economic assistance in return for negotiating a withdrawal; and the Syrians, initially battered and nearly broken by the Israelis in Lebanon, turned to the Soviet Union, who were more than willing to supply weapons, ammunition, economic assistance, and training.[41] With strong backing from the Soviet Union, the Syrians believed they no longer needed to pursue a peace agreement.[42]

Finally, in April 1983, Secretary of State Shultz traveled to the Middle East with a mandate from President Reagan to secure a peace agreement between Israel and Lebanon. Israel was willing at this point to concede to the US' demands for a peace agreement due to the casualties it was suffering in Lebanon and the loss of domestic support for the occupation, that resulted from the Sabra and Shatila massacres.[43] Lebanon was weary of making a deal because it feared signing any agreement with Israel would lead to its banishment from the Arab League, much like what had happened to Egypt after it agreed to the Camp David Peace Accords.[44] With strong assurances from Secretary Shultz that the US would remain involved in Lebanon, and with few other options, the Lebanese Government accepted the peace agreement, which established a diplomatic relationship with Israel and called for the withdrawal of both Israeli and Syrian forces from Lebanon.[45]

Predictably, the Syrians rejected the peace agreement, but through back channels, the Secretary of State had been assured by Saudi Arabia and the Soviet Union that the Syrians would withdrawal as soon as the Israelis did.[46] Colonel Mead, the Commander of the 22nd MAU, believed when he was replaced by the 24th MAU on 30 May 1983 that there was still a strong possibility that the US plan to negotiate the full withdrawal of Israeli and Syrian forces from Lebanon could still succeed.[47] Secretary Shultz was relying on the Israelis to continue the threat of permanent occupation as leverage to convince the Syrians to go along with the 17 May Agreement. Unfortunately, circumstances on the ground made it impossible for the Israelis to maintain their positions in the Shouf Mountains, and they openly began to discuss the possibility of a partial withdrawal to the Awali River. Once this occurred, on 4 September 1983, the Syrians no longer had any motivation to withdrawal their forces from Lebanon.[48] Hafez al Assad, the President of Syria, believed that the Syrians now had the upper-hand, and that with Soviet and Iranian backing he could continue to use both the Druze faction and Syrian troops within Lebanon to further undermine Israel, the US, and the Maronite Christian Government of Amin Gemayel.[49]

The US should have taken this opportunity to once again reassess the grand strategy for Lebanon. The questions that needed to be answered were: Was the US willing to use its considerable military might to force the Syrians to withdrawal from Lebanon? If it did, could it also use political pressure to force the withdrawal of Israel? With the Druze firmly in the Syrian Camp and actively attacking Lebanese and Israeli Forces, was there any chance of political reconciliation? Was it possible for the US to use military force against the Syrians and still keep the support of moderate Arab states such as Saudi Arabia, Jordan, and Egypt? Would the US' partners in the Multi-National Force; France, Italy, and Great Britain, support the use of overwhelming military force? Did the strong presence of the Soviet Union in Syria change the entire calculus?

While none of the answers to these questions were straight forward, what should have been plainly obvious to all of the decision makers within the US was that there was absolutely no chance the US could achieve any of its strategic objectives as long as the Pentagon, Department of State, National Security Council, and Congress remained at odds. Success in Lebanon required an understanding that a political agreement could not be reached without the credible threat of military force, but at the same time, military force had to be discriminately used at appropriate times to modify the behavior of the Syrians and anti-Government factions within Lebanon. Poorly conceived or ill-timed application, of military force had the potential to undermine the political process. Unfortunately, as has been previously discussed in chapter 3, the structure of the US Government does not allow for this type of closely coordinated effort between the diplomats and the military. This structural flaw led to the failure in Lebanon, and later in a similar situation, presented itself again in Iraq, as will be demonstrated in the next chapter.

Disagreement over What Needs to be Done and How to do it

A lack of recognition of how the United States' actions would affect political reconciliation led directly to a lack of consensus about what needed to be done and how to do it. These disagreements erupted into personality disputes between the Secretary of State and the Secretary of Defense, which in turn polarized the National Security Council and paralyzed it from fulfilling its assigned responsibilities. Following the Israeli's retreat from the Shouf Mountains to the Awali River, the Druze Militia and the LAF clashed over who would fill their positions. As the fighting raged, it became clear that the Druze, supported and armed by the Syrians, had the upper hand in the conflict. Special Negotiator Robert McFarland convinced the National Security Council that if the Druze were able to capture the key town of Suq Al Gharb, they would control the high ground over looking Beirut and the International Airport, which would place the Marines stationed at the airport in even greater danger.[50]

National Security Decision Directive 103

On 10 September 1983, President Reagan declared, through National Security Decision Directive 103, that ensuring Suq Al Gharb did not fall to the Anti-Lebanese Forces was vital to the self-defense of the Multi National Force. This Decision Directive is important for two reasons, first, the directive provided guidance from the President to his staff on what was to be considered US vital interests in Lebanon. Second, the Decision Directive changed the Rules of Engagement (ROE) to allow US Forces to use air strikes and naval gunfire to defend the town.[51] However, there were considerable caveats placed on the military commanders before such actions could be taken. Namely, the MAU Commander, Colonel Timothy Geraghty, had to declare that Suq Al Gharb was in imminent danger of being over-run, the enemy was non-Lebanese, and the request had to originate from the Lebanese Government. In reality, there was no way for the Marine Amphibious Commander at the International Airport to know if Suq Al Gharb was in imminent danger or if those attacking the town were non-Lebanese (i.e. Syrian).[52]

The caveats placed on National Security Decision Directive 103, were a symptom of the larger dysfunction within the Reagan Administration and the internal conflicts that had developed between the State Department and the Department of Defense. Each organization had its own view on the utility of military forces in Lebanon and each fought to persuade President Reagan to follow their path; the resulting lack of "consistency and continuity" ensured that there could never be a grand strategy.[53]

State Department versus Department of Defense

Secretary of State Shultz was the most ardent and vocal supporter of Marine involvement in the Multi National Force.[54] For Shultz the presence of the Marines represented the United States' commitment to Lebanon and the entire region. As a diplomat, he was keenly aware that the solution to Lebanon's problems could only be found in political reconciliation, not military action.[55] However, as a seasoned diplomat, he also understood that the credible threat of military force was the strongest leverage he had against Syria. The problem was that with the Marines hunkered down at the International Airport, their credibility as a fighting force was weakened each time they were attacked and failed to respond. Shultz expected three things from the military: initially, he advocated a "presence" mission to help the Lebanese military deter any further outbreak of sectarian violence. When violence did erupt, as he knew it would, he expected a credible threat of force from the Marines and the Navy, to punish those causing problems and compel them to stop their activities. Finally, recognizing that his prized diplomatic effort, (the 17 May Agreement) could be jeopardized by the Syrians, he expected the military to prevent any direct Syrian involvement in Lebanon. In his view, "diplomacy not backed by military strength is ineffectual. Leverage, as well as goodwill is required. Power and diplomacy are not alternatives. They must go together."[56]

At the Department of Defense, Secretary Casper Weinberger had opposed the use of United States Marines from the very beginning.[57] He determined independently that diplomatic efforts were futile, and therefore, United States Troops should not be put into the middle of a civil war that had the potential of spreading into a regional conflict between Israel and Syria.[58] Weinberger sensed early on that the Israelis had overstretched their resources and would be forced to withdrawal.[59] He also believed that the Syrians would never leave Lebanon unless forced to do so. As a pragmatist, Weinberger knew that neither Congress nor the American people would support a war with Syria over Lebanon, because Lebanon did not fit the definition of a vital US interest in any rational calculation.[60] Furthermore, Secretary Shultz's original desire for simply, a presence, of United States Forces particularly disturbed Weinberger because he could not convert, a presence, into a clearly understood and articulated mission with objectives, which he could then assign to his forces.[61]

Beyond their policy differences and their beliefs on how the military should be employed in Lebanon, Shultz and Weinberger had a long history of conflict, which stemmed all the way back to the Nixon Administration, when Shultz was the Director of the Office of Management and Budget and Weinberger was his Deputy.[62] Their relationship was so acrimonious that another Nixon Cabinet Member noted the two refused to even talk politely to each other.[63] Inside the Reagan Administration, many wondered whether their "need to prevail in the administration's internal bureaucratic

tug-of war," took priority over the nation's best interest.[64] Due to the manner in which President Reagan crafted policy, neither of them ever really won. Shultz was successful in initially convincing the President to employ the Marines and he also managed to convince the President that they must stay, even after the 23 October terrorist bombing.[65] Weinberger, however, succeeded at ensuring that the ROE were so stringent that the Marines could not be used for anything other than the officially stated, presence mission.[66] Whether it was because of past history and personality conflicts or simply different beliefs, grand strategy in Lebanon did not exist to a large degree because Shultz and Weinberger could not find common ground.

The National Security Council versus Defense and State

The National Security Council during Lebanon was led first by William Clark and then by Robert McFarlane. Secretary Schultz and Secretary Weinberger considered both to be overly militaristic and constantly pushing the President to use military force.[67] On the State Department side, Shultz did not like the way the National Security Council was run, saying in his memoir, "time and again, I had seen White House and NSC [National Security Council] staff members all too ready to take matters into their own hands, usurping power and authority that was not theirs and going off on their own."[68] At one point during negotiations for the 17 May Agreement, National Security Advisor Clark sent his then deputy, Robert McFarland, on a secret trip to the Middle East to conduct back-channel diplomacy. When Shultz found out about it, he went to President Reagan and said, "when you do this, you undercut me ...[and] you send a message to Middle East leaders that if they don't like what they hear from the Secretary of State, they can use another channel, a back channel to the White House."[69] Unfortunately for Shultz, his conversation did little to change the fact that the National Security Advisor, for no other reason than daily proximity to the President, is able to over-ride the advice of both the Department of Defense and the State Department.[70] Shultz and Weinberger believed that they continually had to fight to ensure that the National Security Council stayed in its lane of coordination and allowed the State Department to conduct operations.[71] In defense of the National Security Council, they may have thought that because the State Department and the Department of Defense refused to cooperate with each other, the only way to carry out the President's desires was to run things themselves.

Whether the National Security Advisor and his staff were blatantly attempting to usurp power, or less nefariously, they were simply filling a need to carry out the President's desires, which Defense and State refused to cooperate on, the affect was exactly the same. The diplomatic, informational, military, and economic policies aimed at stabilizing Lebanon and creating the conditions, within which political reconciliation could occur were never integrated into a grand strategy.[72] As a result, both allies and enemies of the US perceived the internal conflict within the Reagan Administration, which in turn led them to believe they could openly challenge the Marine Forces on the ground or simply wait them out.[73]

If the Strategy is not Working: "Americanize" it

As it became clear the Lebanese Government was failing to take the steps necessary to build the political reconciliation, there was a tendency to attempt to "Americanize" the strategy. The original intent of the Multi-National Force in Beirut was to provide breathing space for the Geyamel Government to conduct negotiations with its internal rivals and form a stable government that could stand on its own. The US was intent on remaining neutral in the conflict and believed that showing favoritism to one faction over the other would hurt the political reconciliation process. There was also a fear that showing favoritism would undermine the effort to achieve a US brokered peace throughout the Middle East. Over the course of 1982 and 1983, the strategy of remaining neutral was undermined first by the agreement to train the LAF, and then by National Security Decision Directive 103.

By agreeing to train the LAF and provide them American uniforms, Colonel Tom Stokes, the Commander of the 24th MAU, inadvertently undermined their position as a neutral peacekeeping force.[74] Fearing his Marines would become complacent, with little to occupy their time, Stokes accepted a request from the Government of Lebanon to train select groups of the LAF.[75] In theory, this made perfect sense. In order for the US to leave, they would eventually have to be replaced by a professional Lebanese Army comprised of more than just factional militias loyal to their individual religious sects. Unfortunately, the Lebanese Army was never able to achieve this status, primarily because President Geyamel was unwilling to negotiate with his Druze and Muslim adversaries.[76] Although the Marines made great progress with the Lebanese Army, it was ultimately viewed as nothing more than a well trained and supplied Phalange Militia.[77] Thus, the agreement to train the Lebanese Army was the first step in "Americanizing" the political reconciliation process and "inextricably linked the intentionally visible Marines to the fate of the LAF and, by extension, identified the Marines and their government completely with the fate of the Gemayel government."[78]

National Security Decision Directive 103 represented the ultimate attempt by the US Government to Americanize the reconciliation process. After it was put in place on 10 September 1983, Special Negotiator McFarlane put immense pressure on the new MAU Commander, Colonel Geraghty, to approve the use of naval gunfire in support of LAF fighting to maintain control of Suq Al Gharb.[79] President Reagan added to the political pressure by directly phoning Geraghty on 13 September 1983. It is reported that he said, "hey pal, you have the 6th Fleet sitting out there, don't hesitate to use them."[80] At the same time Geraghty felt the opposite pressure from the military chain of command. The European Command, the Joint Chiefs of Staff, and ultimately, the Secretary of Defense were all in strong agreement that shelling the Shouf would have no enduring strategic value and would only endanger United States Forces further by removing any doubt as to whether the Multi-National Force was going to remain neutral peacekeepers.[81] Finally, on 19 September 1983, Geraghty relented and gave the approval for the USS John Rogers and the USS Virginia to use their 5-inch guns to pound the enemy positions around Suq Al Gharb with over 350 rounds.[82] His decision was based on two critical factors: first, the Marines at the International Airport were receiving greater amounts of shelling from the Shouf Mountains. Second, Russian-made T-55 Tanks were confirmed to be in the area of Suq Al Gharb, which clearly indicated direct Syrian involvement.[83]

The American shelling of Suq Al Gharb was necessitated by the perceived inability of the Lebanese Government to achieve political reconciliation on its own. It was believed that if the Americans could just provide the Lebanese Government with a little more backing, President Geyamel would have the legitimacy needed to force the factions into a negotiated settlement.[84] Certainly an argument can be made that it may have succeeded if the military actions were tightly coordinated with diplomatic, economic, and information operations. Unfortunately, because such a grand strategy did not exist, the shelling of the Shouf, "actually had the opposite effect of prejudicing that strategy to the point where a new, much more confrontational military strategy was unavoidable."[85]

Military Roles versus Political Objectives: lack of Congruency

No analysis of Lebanon would be complete without a discussion on the lack of congruency between the overarching United States' Foreign Policy objectives and the objectives the Marines were asked to achieve. Following the September shelling of Suq Al Gharb, Secretary of Defense Casper Weinberger approached President Reagan with a proposal to remove the United States Marines from the International Airport, where they were unable to protect themselves, and place them off-shore on Naval vessels, where they would be less vulnerable and yet still able to respond if the circumstances required it.[86] The State Department countered that if the Marines left the airport, it would look like the Americans were cutting and running.[87] President Reagan agreed with the State Department and decided to keep the Marines at the International Airport.[88] On 23 October 1983, a yellow Mercedes truck, penetrated the barriers around the Marine Headquarters, drove into the lobby and exploded, collapsing the building and leading to the deaths of 241 United States Marines. Almost immediately, a sense began to immerge within the US that the Marines were sent to Lebanon without a clear mission; they lacked adequate support, and did not have the means or authority to properly defend themselves.[89] The morning after the bombing, Senator Ernest Hollings echoed this sentiment during an interview on the Today Show saying, "If they were sent there to fight, there are too few. If they were sent there to die, there were too many."[90] Under pressure to explain what happened, Weinberger appointed Retired Admiral Robert Long to lead an independent inquiry into the bombing. The inquiry was given wide latitude and the conclusions it reached went well beyond simple military matters. Specifically on the relationship between the role the military was supposed to perform, and the larger United States Foreign Policy objectives, the commission found:

> By the end of September 1983, the situation in Lebanon had changed to the extent that not one of the initial conditions upon which the mission statement was premised was still valid. The environment clearly was hostile. The assurances the Government of Lebanon had obtained from the various factions were obviously no longer operative as attacks on the USMNF came primarily from extra-legal militias. Although USMNF actions could properly be classified as self-defense and not "engaging in combat", the environment could no longer be characterized as peaceful. The image of the USMNF, in the eyes of the factional militias, had become pro-Israeli, pro-Phalange, and anti-Muslim. After the USMNF engaged in direct fire support of the LAF, a significant portion of the Lebanese populace no longer considered the USMNF a neutral force.[91]

Although the Long Commission found that there could be no conclusive link between the US providing direct fire support to LAF and the terrorist bombing, what was clear was that Marines did not have the force composition or ROE that would have allowed them to accomplish the United States' three stated objectives: deter violence, compel an end to the ongoing violence, and deny Syria and Syrian-backed opposition the ability to undermine the Government of Lebanon.[92]

Grand Strategy

The remaining questions are: Would a properly formulated flexible grand strategy, which combined all of the elements of national power: diplomacy, information, military force, and economic assistance have made a difference in Lebanon? Would it have allowed the Marines to accomplish the goals set forth by the State Department? Clearly any answer to those questions would be purely conjecture; however, to Donald Rumsfeld who replaced Robert McFarlane as the Special Negotiator to the Middle East, just weeks before the 23 October terrorist attack, the Department of Defense's continuous unwillingness to work with the Department of State in formulating a grand strategy was inexcusable.[93] For Rumsfeld, Secretary Shultz, and National Security Advisor McFarlane, "Military leaders consistently hid behind narrow interpretations of the military mission and ROE constraints in order to avoid the military's larger strategic responsibility."[94] Rumsfeld believed that the regional experts and generals, who advised against direct military intervention, did not understand what "the lethality of modern, sophisticated weapons in the hands of a well-trained military force like the Sixth Fleet, could do."[95] These two beliefs, that the Department of Defense had sabotaged US Foreign Policy objectives in Lebanon, and that the generals and regional experts did not understand what modern, sophisticated weapons could achieve, would lead directly, as we will see in the next chapter, to the chaos that ensued after the 2003 US invasion of Iraq.

Notes

1. Ralph A. Hallenbeck, *Military Force as an Instrument of US Foreign Policy* (New York: Praeger, 1991). Dr. Hallenbeck holds a Ph.D. in Political Science from Pennsylvania State University as was the Chief of the Strategic Plans and Policy Division on the Army Staff. In 1979, while serving at the US European Command as the Chief of Operations and Plans, he was "personally involved in planning, supporting, and controlling the activities of the Marine and Naval Forces in Lebanon." From About the Author, in Military Force as an Instrument of US Foreign Policy.

2. Lawrence A. Yates, *The US Military's Experience in Stability Operations, 1789-2000* (Ft Leavenworth, KS: Combat Institute Studies Press, 2005), 80.

3. CB20120313E0001, CIA Analyst, Interview by Charles Bris-Bois, 13 March 2012, Quantico.

4. CB20120313E0001, CIA Analyst.

5. George Schultz, *Turmoil and Triumph: Diplomacy, Power, and the Victory of the American Ideal* (New York: Charles Scribner's Sons, 1993), 429.

6. Hallenbeck, *Military Force as an Instrument of US Foreign Policy*, 3.

7. B. J. Odeh, *Lebanon Dynamics of Conflict* (London: Zed Books, 1985), 173-188.

8. Odeh.

9. Odeh.

10. CB20120313E0001, CIA Analyst, Interview.

11. Odeh, *Lebanon Dynamics of Conflict*, 184.

12. CB20120313E0001, CIA Analyst, Interview.

13. Richard A. Gabriel, *Operation Peace for Galilee: The Israeli-PLO War in Lebanon* (New York: Hill and Wang, 1984).

14. Hallenbeck, *Military Force as an Instrument*, 7. See also John Laffin, *The War of Desperation: Lebanon 1982-85* (London: Osprey, 1985); Benis Frank, *US Marines in Lebanon 1982-1984* (Washington, DC: Government Printing Office, 1987) for further analysis of the Marines' initial mission to evacuate the PLO from Beirut.

15. Hallenbeck., 13.

16. CB20120313E0001, CIA Analyst, Interview.

17. Col. Timothy J. Geraghty, USMC (Ret.), *Peacekeepers At War: Beirut 1983-The Marine Commander Tells His Story* (Washington, DC: Potomac Books, 2009), 7.

18. CB20120313E0001, CIA Analyst, Interview.

19. Geraghty, *Peacekeepers*, 5.

20. Peter Huchthausen, *America's Splendid Little Wars: A Short History of US Military Engagements: 1975-2000* (New York: Viking, 2003), 51.

21. Huchthausen, *America's Splendid Little Wars*, 51.

22. Huchthausen, 52.

23. Col James M. Mead, USMC, Interview by Benis M. Frank, Camp Geiger, January, 13, 1983, Benis M. Frank Papers, Gray Research Center Archives, Marine Corps University Library, Quantico, Va.

24. Huchthausen, *America's Splendid Little Wars,* 53.

25. Huchthausen, 54.

26. Col Timothy J. Geraghty, USMC, Interview by Benis M. Frank, on board USS Iwo Jima, November 21 1983, Benis M. Frank Papers, Gray Research Center Archives, Marine Corps University Library, Quantico, Va.

27. Geraghty, USMC, Interviews.

28. See full discussion on Suq al Gharb in the Chapter 4 sub-section entitled: If the Strategy is not working "Americanize" it.

29. Huchthausen, *America's Splendid Little Wars,* 57.

30. Huchthausen.

31. Geraghty, *Peacekeepers,* 168.

32. Huchthausen, *America's Splendid Little Wars,* 58.

33. These four reasons are derived from Ralph Hallenbeck's thesis in, *Military Force as an Instrument of US Foreign Policy.* Hallenbeck actually gave six reasons, but for the purposes of this paper, the four most relevant have been chosen and re-ordered by priority. Hallenbeck's original thesis was intended to show that the six main reasons why the US mission in Lebanon failed were the same six reasons that led to the failed mission in Vietnam. This paper attempts to take that argument one step further and by using four of his six reasons show that they can also be used to explain the initial failure of the military mission in Iraq in 2003. For more information see Hallenbeck, *Military Force as an Instrument of US Foreign Policy.*

34. Col James M. Mead, USMC, Speech to Naval War College, September 14, 1983, Benis M. Frank Papers, Gray Research Center Archives, Marine Corps University Library, Quantico, Va.

35. CB20120313E0001, CIA Analyst, Interview.

36. Col James M. Mead, USMC, Interview by Benis M. Frank, Camp Geiger, January, 13, 1983, Benis M. Frank Papers, Gray Research Center Archives, Marine Corps University Library, Quantico, Va.

37. Mead, USMC, Interviews.

38. Sandra Mackey, *Lebanon: Death of a Nation* (New York: Gogdon and Weed, 1989), 181-185.

39. Casper Weinberger, *Fighting for Peace: Seven Critical Years in the Pentagon* (New York: Warner Books, 1990), 151.

40. Hallenbeck, *Military Force as an Instrument,* 49-50. Hallenbeck uses articles from the both the *Washington Post* and the *New York Times* to support this assertion. "Lebanon: The Strain is Evident," *Los Angeles Times,* 6 February 1983, 28; "Arens Charges Weinberger Bias, Radio Reports," *Washington Post,* 26 February 83, 13.

41. Shultz, *Turmoil and Triumph,* 196. The Soviet Union went so far as to station technicians in Syria to man their anti-aircraft defenses.

42. Weinberger, *Fighting for Peace,* 56-57.

43. Mead, Speech to Naval War College.

44. Shultz, *Turmoil and Triumph,* 197.

45. Schultz.

46. Weinberger, *Fighting for Peace,* 155.

47. Col James M. Mead, USMC, Interview II, by Benis M. Frank, Marine Corps Head Quarters, May 5, 1984, Benis M. Frank Papers, Gray Research Center Archives, Marine Corps University Library, Quantico, Va.

48. Col Timothy J. Geraghty, USMC, Interview by Benis M. Frank, on board USS Iwo Jima, November 21 1983, Benis M. Frank Papers, Gray Research Center Archives, Marine Corps University Library, Quantico, Va.

49. For more in-depth explanations of the politics surrounding the 17 May Agreement, see all of Shultz, *Turmoil and Triumph,* Chapters 14 and 15.

50. Lou Cannon and Carl M. Cannon, *Reagan's Disciple: George W. Bush's Troubled Quest for a Presidential Legacy* (New York: Public Affairs, 2008), 147.

51. Geraghty, Interview by Benis M. Frank.

52. Geraghty, *Peacekeepers at War,* 64-72.

53. Geraghty, 172.

54. Shultz, *Turmoil and Triumph,* 80.

55. Schultz, Chapter 15. Secretary Shultz saw the 17 May Agreement as the only reasonable means to achieve lasting peace.

56. Schultz, 138.

57. Casper Weinberger and Gretchen Roberts, *In The Arena: A Memoir of the 20th Century* (Lanham, MD: National Book Network, 2001), 312.

58. Weinberger and Roberts.

59. Weinberger, *Fighting for Peace,* 135-174.

60. Weinberger.

61. The Weinberger Doctrine, first presented at the National Press Club on 28 November 1984, was drawn largely from his experience as Secretary of Defense during Lebanon. Within the Doctrine, Weinberger laid out six principles that should be met prior to committing combat forces. First, there has to be a vital national interest. Second, there has to be a commitment to winning. Third, there should be clearly defined political and military objectives. Fourth, when the objectives change, as they inevitably do, we must go back and ask, "is this conflict still a vital national interest that requires us to fight?" Fifth, there must be a reasonable expectation of support from Congress and the American people. Sixth, commitment of combat forces should be the last resort. Interestingly, after Lebanon, President Reagan held to this doctrine, with only one exception, which was the air strikes against Libya in April of 1986.

62. Cannon and Cannon, *Reagan's Disciple,* 141.

63. Cannon and Cannon.

64. Hallenbeck, *Military Force as an Instrument,* 99.

65. Shultz, *Turmoil and Triumph,* 229.

66. Geraghty, Interview by Benis M. Frank.

67. Weinberger, *Fighting for Peace,* 159.

68. Shultz, *Turmoil and Triumph,* 321.

69. Schultz, 313.

70. Weinberger, *In the Arena,* 351.

71. This propensity for the National Security Council to want to conduct operations rather than simply act as advisors led directly to the Iran-Contra Arms for Hostages Scandal, which came to light in 1986. See Shultz, *Turmoil and Triumph,* 843-845; Weinberger, *In the Arena,* 299.

72. Geraghty, *Peacekeepers at War,* 172-173.

73. Geraghty.

74. Eric Hammel, The Root: The Marines in Beirut, August 1982-February 1984 (St Paul: Zenith Press, 2005), 57. Hammel asserts that Col Stokes made the decision to train the LAF. "The decision to honor the Lebanese Ministry of Defense's request to train and upgrade the LAF was casual, an attempt by the MAU commander concerned over the effects of garrison life on his highly motivated troops, an effort to allow Marines largely trapped within the BIA to kill time by doing one of the things Marines do best: training....In a way, it was among the most crucial decisions taken during the entire Marine experience in Beirut."

75. Frank, *US Marines in Lebanon 1982-1984,* 40. Frank states that the plan was proposed by the Joint Chiefs of Staff on November 11, 1982, but only "if it did not interfere with the Marines' basic mission."

76. CB20120313E0001, CIA Analyst, Interview.

77. Col Geraghty stated, "The LAF had shown a cohesiveness that reflected the makeup of the professional balance that reflected the Lebanese people. . . . So the cohesiveness of the LAF that handled themselves through two very difficult military operations in a period of a month, that was really an army that wasn't a year old, was quite phenomenal." Geraghty, Interview by Benis M. Frank.

78. Hammel, *The Root,* 57.

79. Mead, Interview II, by Benis M. Frank.

80. Mead, Speech to Naval War College.

81. Geraghty, Interview by Benis M. Frank.

82. Geraghty.

83. Geraghty.

84. CB20120313E0001, CIA Analyst, Interview.

85. Hallenbeck, *Military Force as an Instrument,* 97.

86. Weinberger, *Fighting for Peace,* 161.

87. Geraghty, Interview by Benis M. Frank.

88. The debate regarding whether or not to move the Marines off-shore was also influenced by the April 18, 1983 car bombing of the American Embassy in Beirut, which killed 61 employees, including 17 Americans. See, Benis Frank, *US Marines in Lebanon,* 59-60.

89. Peter Huchthausen, *America's Splendid Little Wars: A Short History of US Military Engagements: 1975-2000* (New York: Viking, 2003), 61.

90. Cannon and Cannon, *Reagan's Disciple,* 150.

91. Report of the DOD Commission on Beirut International Airport Terrorist Act, October 23, 1883.

92. Geraghty, *Peacekeepers at War,* 139.

93. Hallenbeck, *Military Force as an Instrument,* 146.
94. Hallenbeck.
95. Hallenbeck.

Chapter 5
Iraq Case Study

Understanding How the United States Became Involved

Containment

At the conclusion of the 1991 Gulf War, Saddam Hussein remained in power with his highly trained Republican Guard largely intact. The decision made by the first Bush Administration to not destroy the Republican Guard and remove Saddam Hussein, meant that the US would have to remain in the Gulf region to maintain and enforce the Northern and Southern No-Fly Zones designed to protect the Shia in the South and the Kurds in the North from Saddam's brutality.[1] Paul Wolfowitz, the Undersecretary for Defense Policy at the time, was one of the few who openly argued against the Chairman of the Joint Chiefs of Staff, Colin Powell, insisting that the US was passing up an opportunity to remove a proven tyrant.[2] Dick Cheney, the Secretary of Defense, sided with Powell, believing that a now weakened Saddam Hussein could be contained.

For over a decade, from 1991 until the invasion in 2003, containment largely worked. During the Clinton Administration, the Iraqi Armed Forces made multiple attempts to harass the Kurds and Shia, who were under a blanket of protection provided by the American-led coalition of French, British, and American aircraft. The Iraqis also attempted to harass the aircraft patrolling the No-Fly Zone, which resulted in counter attacks against the anti-aircraft batteries and other designated priority targets.[3] While the US and its coalition partners were not at war with Iraq, there was a persistent low-level conflict that extended throughout this period of containment.

Iraq Liberation Act

Not everyone was happy with the policy of containment, having left government after the first Bush Administration to become the Dean of The Nitze School of Advanced International Studies at Johns Hopkins University, Wolfowitz joined the Project for a New American Century in the mid-1990s. The Project for a New American Century was a group of Pro-Israeli, conservative Republicans, which called for the US to change its policy of containment toward Iraq and actively seek to overthrow Saddam's regime.[4] Many within the group believed that by replacing Saddam with a democratic government that recognized Israel's right to exist would have two major affects: first, it would remove one of the Israel's primary threats in the region, and second, members of the Project for the New American

Century believed that removing Saddam could be a catalyst to changing the entire Middle East.[5] In January 1998, the group presented President Clinton with a letter laying out their argument for why containment was failing. The authors, which included Richard Cheney, Donald Rumsfeld, Paul Wolfowitz, Lewis Libby and Elliot Abrams, pointed out that the policy depended on the cooperation of allies to maintain the sanctions, and on Saddam's willingness to allow inspectors access to sites throughout the country.[6] On 31 October 1998, President Clinton signed into law the Iraq Liberation Act, making regime change the official policy of the US.[7]

In response to this new threat from the US, Saddam kicked all of the United Nations (UN) Weapons Inspectors out of the country. This action in turn led to the launching of Operation Desert Fox, in December of 1998 by the US. Richard Butler, the Australian head of the UN Weapons Inspection Team, provided the US with a list of 100 possible sites that he believed Saddam may be hiding 32,000 chemical munitions, 4,000 tons of chemical precursors, and 550 mustard gas bombs that were unaccounted for.[8] From a tactical perspective, Operation Desert Fox was a success, with Tomahawk Missiles and air-dropped ordnance hitting 97 of the 100 targets.[9] From a strategic perspective, Operation Desert Fox was less successful, in that it created problems for the US by fracturing the coalition that had been solidly behind punishing Saddam. France pulled their aircraft from the coalition and no longer supported the enforcement of the No-Fly Zones.[10] China called for a review of the sanctions, and Saudi Arabia and Turkey disavowed support for the United States' operation.[11] Saudi Arabia and Turkey opposed Operation Desert Fox largely for the same reasons they opposed expanding the US mandate in 1991, namely they were concerned with the second and third order effects the operation could have on their internal domestic politics, especially, if the operation led to the collapse of the Saddam regime. The Arabs told General Anthony Zinni, Commander US Central Command, "An implosion is going to cause chaos...You're going to have to go in...do you have a plan?"[12] This fracturing of the alliance of nations opposed to Saddam Hussein would create significant problems for George W. Bush and his administration when it attempted to convince the UN to authorize war against Iraq once again in 2003.

George W. Bush Administration

After Operation Desert Fox, the US returned to the strategy of responding to Iraq's actions with limited air strikes. In August of 2001, United States Marine Corps Commandant, General Jim Jones, sent the Joint Chiefs of Staff and Secretary of Defense, Donald Rumsfeld, a memorandum critiquing the tit-for-tat approach being taken in response to Iraq's provocations. Jones believed that the approach was no longer working and that it was actually having the negative effect of alienating many within the Arab world. Continuing to respond with limited attacks by our aircraft, Jones wrote in the memorandum, "is a high risk strategy without clear objectives or a discernable end state...the effects it is having on our Arab allies is at odds with the risk we are taking."[13] It is obvious from the memorandum that Jones believed that the time had come for a new strategy in Iraq, however, he does not lay out in the memorandum what he thinks the new strategy should be. On 10 September 2001, just one day before the 9/11 terrorist attacks, Secretary Rumsfeld responded by saying, "I am working the problem and I certainly agree with your concern."[14] General Jones did not need to convince Undersecretary of Defense Wolfowitz or the number three-man in the Pentagon, Douglas Feith. Both men were ardent supporters of the Iraq Liberation Act, and believed that the US was not doing enough to fulfill its stated policy objective of removing Saddam Hussein from power.[15] Just days after the 9/11 terrorist attacks, Wolfowitz proposed to the President that Iraq should be one of the first nations attacked in the new War on Terror.[16] While President Bush agreed that the US had to do more than just attack Osama Bin Laden in Afghanistan, he believed they must first deal with the Taliban. On 20 September 2001, he told British Prime Minister Tony Blair, "We must deal with [the Taliban] first. But when we have dealt with Afghanistan, we must come back to Iraq."[17]

Phase I Operations

President Bush asked Secretary of Defense Rumsfeld immediately to begin reviewing options for military action in Iraq. After the 9/11 terrorist attacks, President Bush appointed retired General Wayne Downing, the former head of Special Operations Command, to be the Deputy National Security Advisor for Combating Terrorism.[18] With the backing of Undersecretary of Defense Paul Wolfowitz and Lewis "Scooter" Libby, Vice President Dick Cheney's Chief of Staff, Downing worked with Ahmed Chalabi, the leader of the Iraqi National Congress, to revise a plan for starting an insurrection to overthrow Saddam and establish the Iraqi National Congress as the interim government. The new plan was based largely on the model that had shown great initial successful in Afghanistan, "Bombing, a modest insertion of Special Forces, plus an uprising."[19]

This was not Chalabi's first interaction with the US Government. The Chalabi family had been one of the wealthiest and most politically connected Shia families in Iraq prior to the revolution in 1958, they were also tightly connected to the Shia religious elite, Ahmed's grandfather is buried in the shrine of Imam Ali in Najaf, "no small honor in the Shia world."[20] When Saddam took power in Iraq, Ahmed and his family initially took refuge in Lebanon, where he married into another prominent and politically connected Lebanese Shia family.[21] Later, Chalabi moved to the US where he received a degree in mathematics from Massachusetts Institute of Technology and a PhD from the University of Chicago, where he first came into contact and built relationships with the Neoconservatives.[22] In the aftermath of the 1991 Gulf War, when it became clear that the opposition groups within Iraq were not able to overthrow Saddam Hussein, Ahmad Chalabi approached the Clinton Administration with a proposal to allow his external dissidents to attempt to oust Saddam from power.[23] Clinton agreed to fund Chalabi through the Central Intelligence Agency and a small base camp was established from which the Iraqi National Congress could operate in the Kurdish-controlled area of Northern Iraq.[24] In March 1995, Chalabi and his Iraqi National Congress fighters launched an insurrection that was quickly quelled. Saddam drove Chalabi's operation out of Iraq and executed 130 captured Iraqi National Congress members.[25] Feeling they had been misled and sensing that Chalabi and his organization were not up to the task, the State Department and the Central Intelligence Agency cut ties with the Iraqi National Congress.[26]

Downing and Chalabi realized that the Iraqi National Congress' initial attempt to overthrow Saddam in 1995 failed because the anticipated popular uprising never materialized. To ensure this did not happen again, planners proposed using Iranian assets for assistance. The Iranians recognized that because of the ethnic make-up of Iraq, replacing Saddam with a Shiite Theocracy would never work, but the Iranians still wanted to influence the creation of the new government.[27] The Iraqi National Congress hoped to safely stage its forces inside the Iranian borders as they prepared for the invasion, and additionally planned on strategic support from the Shia population during the fight to drive out Saddam. To this end, the Office of Foreign Assets Control under the Treasury Department gave the Iraqi National Congress approval to use US funds to establish a liaison office in Tehran, which it did in April of 2001.[28]

> Iran's ruling mullahs considered the outcome of the US-led war with Iraq as a matter of life or death for their regime, but their interests in the current crisis were complex. In principle, the toppling of Saddam Hussein was in Tehran's interest; however, Tehran had a greater interest in the dismemberment of Iraq, so that Tehran might, by capitalizing on its influence over Syria's Allawites and

Lebanon's HizbAllah, consolidate the Shiite belt all the way to the Mediterranean.[29]

In light of Chalabi's past history and fear over Iranian intentions, the Special Envoy to the Middle East, the Joint Chiefs of Staff, and the State Department, voiced strong opposition to Downing's plan, dubbing it "The Bay of Goats," in reference to the Cuban Bay of Pigs fiasco.[30] Recognizing a lack of support within the government for the Iraqi exile option, Rumsfeld tasked the Commander of US Central Command, General Tommy Franks, to develop alternate options. After nearly two years of work, Central Command Planners delivered a concept of operations that met the demands of the Secretary of Defense. The primary requirement was to ensure this proposal was not a duplication of the 1991 war plan, which required six months to move all of the men and material into theater prior to launching the war.[31]

Phase II Operations

For almost a year, Central Command quietly built up forces in the region. To hide their efforts, a new command and control center was built in Qatar inside the climate controlled warehouses that had previously held hundreds of prepositioned M1 Tanks and Bradley Fighting Vehicles, which were now in Kuwait.[32] When the war kicked off, command and control capabilities were double their previous amount, with centers in both Kuwait and Qatar. Pentagon planners overlapped rotation schedules so that carrier strike groups and Air Force Expeditionary Strike Groups would be twice their normal strength leading up to the war, without announcing to the press or the Iraqis that a massive build-up was taking place. In addition, the Army scheduled large exercises to mask the number of combat troops they had in theater.[33]

Preparations for the war were also moving forward on the political front, however, there were disagreements in Washington over whether or not to pursue UN consent. On 10 October 2002, the US House and Senate passed resolutions authorizing the US to remove Saddam Hussein, but urged the State Department to continue pursuing a UN resolution.[34] However, the Joint Chiefs of Staff believed the US should not wait in attacking a known Ansar Al-Islam terrorist training camp in northern Iraq that was making chemical weapons with the intent of using them to attack Europe and the US. Yossef Bodansky, in *The Secret History of the Iraq War,* claims that three terrorists trained at the Ansar Al-Islam facility were caught by Israeli special forces as they tried to enter the Palestinian territories.[35] In subsequent interrogations, the three terrorists revealed a plot to use the chemical agent ricin against targets in Europe, Turkey, and Russia. On 14 January 2003, British agents raided a home in Manchester, and recovered some of the ricin made at the Ansar facility.[36] At that point, Secretary Rumsfeld urged President Bush to authorize an immediate attack to seize or destroy the facility, but Colin Powell and Condoleezza Rice objected, fearing that an attack would undermine efforts to build the coalition and gain UN approval.[37]

Phase III Operations

The main thrust of the attacks, which began on 19 March 2003, were led by the US Army's V Corps in the west, under the Command of Lieutenant General William Wallace and the 1st Marine Expeditionary Force, in the east, led by Lieutenant General James Conway. General Franks designated V Corps the main effort. Major General Buford Blount's 3rd Infantry Division (ID) led the Corps into Iraq. Blount divided his infantry division into three Brigade Combat Teams. After crossing the Euphrates River the Brigade Combat Teams split up and surrounded the southern and western portions of Bagdad.

Responsibility for securing the southern oil fields fell to the 1st Marine Division, under the command of Lieutenant General James Mattis. After securing the oil fields, the Marines raced V Corps to Baghdad where the Marines responsibility was to surround the eastern portion of the city.[38] Both forces encountered pockets of stiff resistance along their routes, most notably, the Marines got tied down in An Nasiriyah, which they originally intended to bypass, but both were still able to make it to the outskirts of Baghdad in a little over four days.[39]

For Lieutenant General David McKiernan, the overall Ground Force Component Commander, the largest risk to his ground forces was the passage of the Karbala Gap. If Saddam was going to use chemical or biological weapons against the coalition, intelligence officials believed it would happen in this region.[40] The original plan called for V Corps to avoid the cities of Najaf and Karbala during their run toward the Karbala Gap, however, the plan changed due to the strong presence of Paramilitary Forces that were coming out of the cities and attacking V Corps' lines of communication. As a result, the 101st Airborne Division, under the command of Major General David Petraeus, was sent into Najaf and Karbala to put down the resistance, while the 3rd ID continued to push north. Severe sand storms and intense fighting stopped 3rd ID's northern progress just south of the Karbala Gap. While the delay was unexpected, it did allow the 3rd ID time to regroup, consolidate, and resupply prior to making the final push to the outskirts of Baghdad.[41] General Wallace recounted after the war:

> For nearly a year, we had recognized collectively that once we were through the Karbala Gap, the fight would not be over until we seized the international airport in Baghdad. The entire fight from Karbala to the airport was considered as one continuous assault, because once we crossed through the gap, we were inside the range of all the artillery that was in support of Baghdad and all the Republican Guard divisions around Baghdad.[42]

Saddam never employed chemical or biological weapons and 3rd ID was able to secure a key bridge across the Euphrates River, allowing the assault to progress faster than was expected. As 3rd ID closed in on Baghdad, General Blount sent the 3rd Brigade Combat Team to circle the city to the west; the 2nd Brigade Combat Team secured the key intersection of Highway 1 and Highway 8 south of the city; and the 1st Brigade Combat Team went directly to Baghdad International Airport.[43]

Baghdad fell on Wednesday, 9 April 2003, with dramatic coverage by the media of a statue of Saddam being pulled down in Firdos Square.[44] In the proceeding days, the 3rd ID, led by Colonel David Perkins' 2nd Brigade Combat Team, made several Thunder Runs, culminating in the 2nd Brigade's capture of the Presidential Palace in the heart of Baghdad.[45] Phase III operations had not gone completely as scripted. However, detailed planning and coordination between the Army, Air Force, and Marines allowed V Corps to adjust on the fly and take advantage of situations as they presented themselves. Unfortunately, the same could not be said for Phase IV operations [46]

Phase IV Operations

For a variety of reasons that will be examined further in this chapter, Phase IV operations never received the same level of attention or detailed planning as Phase III. This does not mean, however, that planning did not occur. General Tommy Franks, the Commander of US Central Command, had a segment of his staff designated to Phase IV planning.[47] The Joint Staff created an organization for Phase IV planning. The State Department tasked members of their organization to do in-depth planning. The National Security Council designated a lead for coordinating post-war planning; and finally, the Undersecretary of Department of Defense for Policy, Douglas Feith, created an organization for planning and conducting post-combat, Phase IV operations in Iraq.[48] Yet largely because of personality conflicts, faulty assumptions, and political infighting there was little cohesion between the various strategies.[49]

Substantial Phase IV planning began just two months before Coalition forces crossed into Iraq. Secretary Rumsfeld brought retired Lieutenant General Jay Garner to the Pentagon in early January 2003 to lead what would become the Office of Reconstruction and Humanitarian Assistance. Garner was the natural choice for the assignment due to his background leading Operation Provide Comfort in 1991.[50] Following the 1991 Gulf War, Garner was tasked with providing humanitarian assistance to 400,000 Kurdish refugees in northern Iraq near the Turkish border.[51] "Without a written operational plan to guide him, Garner demonstrated great operational acumen and remarkable diplomacy to bring the operation to a successful end."[52]

When Garner was brought back in 2003, the primary focus of his new organization centered around immediate reconstruction of vital infrastructure and providing humanitarian relief for the estimated hundreds of thousands of Iraqis who would become refugees during the fighting. A smaller subset of his organization's responsibilities included re-establishing the civil administration, which was required to perform everyday duties such as maintaining electricity sources and collecting garbage. To accomplish these objectives, Garner divided his organization into three pillars: Reconstruction, Humanitarian Assistance, and Civil Administration.[53] Due to the rapid manner in which Baghdad fell and the military's use of precision weapons that avoided damaging critical infrastructure, the extensive planning that had been put into reconstruction and humanitarian assistance was largely unneeded.[54] The pillar requiring the greatest attention, civil administration, had received the least amount of planning focus. It had been made clear to Garner and his staff prior to the invasion that their primary focus was to establish an interim government and hand over responsibility as quickly as possible. To this end, Garner met with a group of selected exiles and local Iraqis at a deserted airfield outside of Tallil on 14 April 2003. Within a week, Garner had settled on an interim government that consisted of two Kurdish leaders, two Shia exiles from London, a Sunni local leader and two Shia leaders who had been living in Iran.[55] Arriving in Baghdad on 21 April 2003, two weeks after the city fell, Garner and his organization could do very little.[56] All of the Iraqi ministries they were attempting to re-establish had been looted, and members of the Office of Reconstruction and Humanitarian Assistance could not regularly venture out into Baghdad due to the increased violence.[57] Four days later, on 24 April, Garner was informed that Ambassador Paul Bremer would replace him on

12 May 2003. The Office of Reconstruction and Humanitarian Assistance would be shut down and replaced by the Coalition Provisional Authority.[58]

Bremer came to Iraq with a clear mandate from the President, the Vice President, the Secretary of State and the Secretary of Defense.[59] Four days before Bremer left Washington for Iraq, he had a one-on-one lunch with President Bush followed by a full meeting of the National Security Council Principals.[60] At lunch with the President, Bremer laid out his belief that democracy could not be established in Iraq until what "[he] called 'Shock Absorbers', a free press, trade unions, political parties, professional organizations" were in place.[61] He told the President it was a marathon and not a sprint. Bush responded by saying, "I understand, and I'm fully committed to bringing representative government to the Iraqi people....We will stay until the job is done."[62] The importance of these words, "we will stay until the job is done," should not be underestimated. It is evident at this point that Bush realized the US could not achieve the stated objective of establishing a representative government by handing Iraq over to the interim government Garner had proposed, which was dominated by exiles and Kurds.[63]

During the National Security Council meeting that followed, Vice President Cheney said, "We're not at a point where representative Iraqi leaders can come forward. They're still too scared. We need a strategy on the ground for the postwar situation we actually have and not the one we wish we had."[64] Secretary of State Powell followed this with, "The president's guidance is to take our time on setting up an Interim Iraqi Administration so what we get is a representative group."[65] Why had the administration done a complete turn-around? Why was it now looking to stay in Iraq for an extended period? Answers to those questions are not entirely clear. What is clear is that with the guidance provided by the President and the National Security Council, Bremer felt confident in implementing the policy of de-Baathification that had been written in Douglas Feith's policy office.

Once on the ground in Iraq, Garner and a host of others advised Bremer that implementing the draconian de-Baathification policy would hamper much of the progress made to re-establish civil administration.[66] Bremer responded by saying that, he, the President, and all of the Principals on the National Security Council understood there might be short-term administrative inconveniences, but it would be valuable in the long-term efforts to ensure Iraq was not threatened by the possibility of Baathists returning to power.[67] On 16 May 2003, Bremer held a press conference at the Baghdad Convention Center where he officially declared General Order 1, removing the top four levels of Ba'athists from leadership positions in the government, schools, and hospitals.[68]

Bremer's arrival in Iraq came at a time of great administrative upheaval and dysfunction. The replacement of The Office of Reconstruction and Humanitarian Assistance by the Coalition Provisional Authority corresponded with General Frank's decision to stand-down General McKiernan's Combined Forces Land Component Commander Headquarters and create a new Combined Joint Task Force to oversee all military units in Iraq.

> When the time came to pick a name one aide suggested CJTF-13, a bit of black humor that pointed to the difficulties ahead. Franks chimed in, "Lets make it CJTF-1369, unlucky cocksuckers."...the episode was indicative of Frank's attitude about the post-war administration.[69]

Franks chose V Corps as the headquarters around which the Combined Joint Task Force was to be built. Further complicating this transition was the fact that V Corps' Commander, General William "Scott" Wallace, was replaced by Lieutenant General Ricardo Sanchez, formerly the Commander of 1st Armored Division, who had just arrived in Iraq. As a result of these changes, Sanchez, a division commander with no previous experience as a corps commander, found himself in charge of the entire coalition.[70]

The ramifications were significant. General McKiernan had been able to cherry-pick the best officers from around the Army for his Combined Forces Land Component Commander staff. When these officers left Iraq and handed over responsibility to the much smaller V Corps staff, they took with them the ability to plan strategic and operational level campaigns, formulate policy, and tap into national-level intelligence. Under McKiernan's Land Component Commander staff, there were several hundred intelligence officers. When Sanchez took over, he was left with fewer than thirty.[71] Equally as damaging was the fact that the V Corps staff had no designated liaison positions for the incoming coalition military partners or for Bremer's new Coalition Provisional Authority interim government.[72] The months of May and June brought tremendous turnover below corps level in the divisions as well.

The Pentagon decided that the policy of Stop-Loss, which limited the transfer of personnel during the war, could be lifted after Phase III operations. The result within 1st Armored Division, which had just arrived in theater to replace the 3rd ID, was that within 45 days, every general officer, the entire division staff, except one, and 70 percent of the battalion commanders were replaced by new soldiers.[73] The loss of continuity in personnel, experience, and cooperate knowledge, contributed significantly to the loss of momentum the US forces suffered over the summer of 2003, which in turn facilitated the rise of the Sunni insurgency.[74]

To make matters worse for both the military and the Coalition Provisional Authority, Rumsfeld cancelled the scheduled deployment of the 1st Cavalry Division on 21 April, believing the deployment was unnecessary because forces were anticipated to withdraw from Iraq in 60 days. According to then Secretary of the Army Thomas White, the Pentagon's pre-war budgetary planning assumed that troop levels would be reduced by 50,000 within the first 90 days after the completion of Phase III, and they would reduce another 50,000 30 days later, essentially leaving a division-plus in Iraq to continue the transition.[75]

Central Command planners made this optimistic planning assumption based on another equally optimistic assumption that 300,000 to 400,000 Iraqi soldiers would be available to replace the United States Forces as they rotated out of the country and that Arab nations would contribute significant forces to Iraq once Phase III was complete. This assumption did not work in practice for several reasons. First, the Iraqi Army followed the guidance they were given via leaflets, airdropped prior to the war, and laid down their weapons and went home.[76] The Iraqi Army essentially disintegrated and it was not clear in the first month after Phase III whether they could be easily reassembled.[77] Second, the US had only budgeted to pay for a single corps of 40,000 Iraqi troops. Even if the Iraqi troops could have been successfully called back to service, it is not clear how they would have been paid, equipped, or trained.[78] Third, the Pentagon and State Department failed to gain support from Arab nations, resulting in a lack of volunteers to provide the necessary peacekeeping forces. General John Abizaid did have offers from several Iraqi Generals to bring back their forces and begin working with the coalition.[79] Walter Slocombe, who would later join the Coalition Provisional Authority to stand up the Iraqi Ministry of Defense, and Ambassador Bremer, however, killed the plan because they believed a Sunni-dominated military would send the wrong message to the Kurdish and Shia populations.[80] Bremer believed the first priority should be, "convincing the Iraqis that we're not going to permit the return of Saddam's instruments of repression...[the new army,] would have to represent the entire nation: Shia, Kurds, and Sunni Arabs."[81]

Rumsfeld agreed with the plan and on 23 May 2003, the Coalition Provisional Authority issued Order No. 2 "Dissolution of Entities."[82]

With wholesale changes in policy, civilian oversight, and military leadership, progress in Iraq ground to a halt in the summer of 2003 and never regained the momentum, it ceded to the insurgents.

Why the United States' Mission in Iraq Initially Failed

> If the intent of operations in Iraq in 2003 was merely 're-gime destruction', which it was not, then the short, decisive warfighting operation of March and April 2003 might in itself have constituted success...In all other respects, it might have been counterproductive.[83]

The following analysis of the United States' invasion of Iraq in 2003 will show that the US failed to employ a grand strategy for four distinct reasons. First, there was a failure to recognize that ultimate success rested almost entirely on political reconciliation between the opposing ethnic groups within Iraqi. Second, this lack of recognition of how US actions would affect political reconciliation led directly to a lack of consensus about what needed to be done and how to do it. These disagreements erupted into personality disputes between Secretary of State Colin Powell and Secretary of Defense Donald Rumsfeld, which in turn polarized the National Security Council and paralyzed it from fulfilling its assigned responsibilities. Third, when the Iraqis proved incapable or unwilling to solve their own problems, there was intense pressure from Washington to "Americanize" the solution. Finally, there was a lack of congruency between the roles the military was given, the objectives it was asked to achieve, and the overarching US Foreign Policy objectives.[84]

Military Mission Wholly Dependent on Political Reconciliation

In the planning for Operation Iraqi Freedom, both the military and civilian planners failed to recognize the important role political reconciliation would play in achieving the United States' objectives. A memorandum dated 29 October 2002, from National Security Advisor Condoleezza Rice to Secretary Rumsfeld and other members of the National Security Council Principals Committee laid out these goals. The memorandum stated the following objectives: "Minimize the risk of WMD [Weapons of Mass Destruction] attack against the United States, US fielded forces, our allies or friends;" and to do it in a manner that, "minimizes the chance of internal instability, fragmentation, and the loss of control of WMD within Iraq." It also identified the need to, "Improve the conditions of life for the Iraqi population;" and finally, "end Iraq as a safe haven for terrorists."[85]

Clearly, if the US was going to minimize the chances of instability and fragmentation, improve quality of life, and prevent Iraq from being a safe haven for terrorists, there would have to be political reconciliation. In the absence of political reconciliation, the Shia, Sunni, and Kurds would naturally compete for dominance, which at best, would result in a low-level civil war. A civil war, by its very nature, would ensure that the objectives were not met.

The only other means the US could use to achieve its stated goals would be to undertake a long-term effort of acting forcefully to impose order and keep factions separated. This approach, in theory, would buy time for the creation of internal security and democratic institutions. However, this course of action, by virtually all legitimate estimates, would require a minimum force of between 300,000 to 500,000 peacekeepers.[86] Even if there had been widespread consensus among the government and the American people that imposing order was the appropriate course of action, it could not have been achieved. The Department of Defense did not have a military large enough to commit anywhere near 300,000 troops on a long-term basis and maintain its commitments in Afghanistan without instituting the draft.[87]

To borrow Senator Earnest Hollings' quotation from the last chapter on Lebanon, Franks should have recognized early on that his plan to leave a division-plus size force in Iraq after the fall of Saddam was nowhere near adequate to complete the mission, and that his plan would be open to the critique, "if they were put there to fight, there were too few. If they were put there to die, they are too many."[88]

The question becomes why Franks and his staff at Central Command abdicated their responsibility to ensure the military campaign matched the overall political objectives? There appear to be three main reasons. First, based off his experience in Vietnam, Franks determined he would not let politics interfere with his military plan. "Franks would tell the civilians to stay the hell out of military matters, and he would keep out of their business."[89] Second, he was under tremendous pressure from Rumsfeld to transform the military and the way it fought wars into lighter, faster, less manpower intensive organization.[90] Finally, in keeping with his policy of staying out of the civilian politicians' business, he trusted the Office of Special Plans in the Pentagon to deliver on their promise that the Office of Reconstruction and Humanitarian Assistance would handle Phase IV operations.[91] Franks made it clear to his subordinate military commanders that they were to "offer only transportation, logistics, and some communications capabilities."[92]

Under normal conditions, the State Department would have played a role in Phase IV operations as well. However, two months before the invasion, the Office of Special Plans, which belonged to the Undersecretary of Defense for Policy, Douglas Feith, drafted a memorandum, which called for the Department of Defense to have complete control of post-war Iraq. The memo was taken straight to the President via the Vice President's office, thus skipping the normal National Security Council debates on its merits. President Bush signed the memo on 20 January 2003, as National Security Presidential Directive (NSPD) 24.[93] To understand how the Office of Special Plans was able to achieve such a feat, a little background on the Neoconservatives who ran the office is required.

Neoconservatives

The Neoconservatives' fundamental belief was that the already secularized Iraq could be turned into a pro-western democracy, which in turn would lead other Arab states in the region to overthrow their repressive regimes.[94] In the Neoconservative narrative, once the old authoritarian regimes were deposed, the underlying causes of Islamic extremism and terrorism would be gone, and moderate Arabs, who also wanted peace with Israel, would come to power.[95]

Michael Harrington, a political science professor at Queens College, first used the term Neoconservative to describe, "liberals he believed were acting as conservatives."[96] Although he used the term in a negative fashion, many former liberals who thought the Democratic Party was not doing enough to oppose Communism embraced it. After the Cold War the group tended to represent those who did not think the US was doing enough to support Israel.[97]

Dr. Leo Stauss and Dr. Albert Wohlstetter, both professors in the political science department at the University of Chicago, are credited with providing the intellectual framework for Neoconservative ideas. Their work heavily influenced two students who would become leading Neoconservatives in the Bush Administration, Richard Perle and Paul Wolfowitz. Stauss was an anti-Communist theorist who taught his students that Winston Churchill's example of standing up to Hitler and fighting against totalitarianism is what all great leaders should aspire to.[98] Wohlstetter was a mathematician who provided the science needed to back those who argued the US needed more nuclear weapons and an Anti-Ballistic-Weapons System to defend against the Communist threat.

In 1969, Dr. Wohlstetter was working with Senator Henry Jackson, a staunch Democrat from Washington State, and a leading proponent of the

64

Anti-Ballistic-Missile Defense System in the Senate. Needing assistance to draft a bill that would authorize the construction of the Anti-Ballistic Missile System, he called on the expertise of two graduate students, Paul Wolfowitz and Richard Perle. The bill passed the Senate 51 to 50, with the Vice President casting the winning vote.[99] Wolfowitz went back to school to finish his doctoral thesis, which centered on the proliferation of nuclear weapons in the Middle East and the need for the US to act preemptively to stop Islamic states from acquiring nuclear weapons. In addition, he emphasized the need to protect vital national interests such as the free access to Middle East oil.[100] Richard Perle stayed in Washington, eventually becoming the Assistant Secretary of Defense for International Security Policy in the Reagan Administration, where he hired Douglas Feith as his Deputy Assistant Secretary.[101]

The three were brought back into government at the beginning of the George W. Bush Administration to act as foreign policy advisors for the campaign. Wolfowitz became the Undersecretary of Defense, Feith, the Undersecretary of Defense for Policy, and Perle was assigned the Chairman of the Defense Policy Board Advisory Committee. Along with their neoconservative foreign policy views, the three men brought with them an association with another mathematician from the University of Chicago, long-time friend Ahmed Chalabi.[102]

In a previously classified document, written on 30 March 2003, during the coalition's first weeks of combat as they marched toward Baghdad, the Office of Special Plans, run by Feith and supported by Wolfowitz, laid out their argument that the new government in Iraq should be led by the Shia. The document said, "this implies breaking with Iraq's history of domination by the Sunni Arab minority—a potentially painful political process."[103] The document went on to say that while there needed to be power sharing between ethnic and sectarian groups, the majority of internal Iraqis were not yet ready to participate in a democratic society. Further, the memorandum outlined two interests, one substantive and one procedural. The substantive interest was in a moderate, pro-western, democratic Iraq. The procedural interest was in gaining broad support for the new government by allowing all Iraqis, including those unfriendly to the west, to participate in forming the government. The later procedural interest allowed the US to be hands off, while the substantive interest required direct US control of the process. The memo concluded that, "The US should not now raise procedural considerations above our substantive goal."[104]

The Special Plans Office convinced the President and the National Security Council Principals to adopt the substantive goal and to form an Iraqi

Interim Authority, which would give an advantage to those who shared the United States' interest in a pro-western free Iraq.[105] The Iraqi Interim Authority would be controlled by the Coalition Provisional Authority (Paul Bremer), and composed of 21 members, one from each of Iraq's 18 provinces, and one from each of Iraq's minority religious and ethnic groups; the Chaldeans, the Assyrians, the Yezidis, and the Turkomen.[106] In theory, this sounded like an attempt to build political reconciliation. In reality, because the members were required to "subscribe to a set of principles," those who did not were left out of the process.[107] Thus, rather than creating reconciliation, the Iraqi Interim Authority was nothing more than a veiled attempt to give the externals and pro-western internals a head-start in forming and running the new Iraqi Government. By excluding those who did not subscribe to the interests of the US, the creation of the Interim Authority guaranteed, "a potentially painful political process," one that would generate greater conflict along sectarian lines rather than reconciliation.

Disagreement over What Needs to be Done and How to Do it

In Iraq, just as it was in Lebanon, political reconciliation was the only means by which political objectives could be achieved, thus avoiding civil war and allowing the US to decrease force presence. However, in a manner similar to what had occurred 20 years earlier in Lebanon, the Pentagon and State Department came to vastly different conclusions on what needed to be done by the Americans. As the next sections will show, these disagreements erupted into personality conflicts between key cabinet members, preventing the two organizations from combining military and diplomatic efforts to form a grand strategy.

Rumsfeld versus Powell

While there were many sources of conflict between the Pentagon and the State Department, the largest was by far Ahmed Chalabi. As referenced above, the 1998 Iraq Liberation Act made regime change in Iraq official US Policy. The Neocons, Perle, Wolfowitz, and Feith, and their Project for a New American Century, believed Chalabi was still the best viable option for making regime change a reality. They brought forward a plan in which the Iraqi National Congress would return to northern Iraq and be officially recognized as the provisional government. Supporters of this plan proposed that the Iraqi National Congress be funded by the $1.5 billion in Iraqi assets that had been frozen by the US Government during the 1991 Gulf war.[108] Ultimately, the Iraq Liberation Act did authorize full funding of the Iraqi National Congress. However, the State Department blocked all but a small portion of the funds.[109]

66

Chalabi's original proposal to the Clinton Administration involved the training of 5,000 Iraqi fighters who would eventually be inserted into an abandoned airfield near Basra. These actions would force Saddam to implement a plan. He could either move against the insurgents, in which case American airpower would be employed, or he could choose to keep his forces closer to Bagdad for protection, in which case, the insurgents would take control of Basra and the southern oil fields thus cutting off the oil revenue Saddam needed to stay in power.[110]

The Clinton Administration rejected the plan largely because of distrust of Chalabi and the Iraqi National Congress within the State Department, and because of the opposition by US Central Command Commander General Anthony Zinni, who told a Senate committee in 1998, "Even if we had Saddam gone, we could end up with fifteen, twenty, or ninety groups competing for power."[111]

Thus, even before Wolfowitz and Feith were to take their prominent positions in Bush's Department of Defense, the arguments over the utility of using Chalabi to carry out America's Foreign Policy had already created deep fissures between them and the State Department. After the President signed NSPD 24, giving the Pentagon full control of post-Saddam Iraq, the State Department attempted to send two of its brightest civil servants to work for the Office of Reconstruction and Humanitarian Assistance. Tom Warrick had led the Future of Iraq Project at the State Department, and was a by-name request from Garner; Megan O'Sullivan was a specialist in ethnic conflict and constitutional design.[112] The Pentagon rejected both because of previous statements each had made that did not fit with the Neoconservative's view of how post-Saddam Iraq should be run.[113] When Secretary Powell found out, he called Secretary Rumsfeld and said, "we can take prisoners too."[114] Clearly, the conflict between the State Department and the Defense Department had now moved beyond the substantive debates over how and when military force should be used. It was now personal and would negatively impact future dealings between the two departments, ensuring that the diplomatic and military efforts were never united into a grand strategy.

Rumsfeld versus the Military

Powell was not the only person with whom Rumsfeld battled and allowed professional differences to turn personal. Inside the Pentagon, Rumsfeld was publicly feuding with the military brass. For years, dating all the way back to his early political career as a Congressman, Rumsfeld had advocated for a more technologically advanced force that could be rapidly deployed. He told President-Elect Bush not to hire him as the Secretary of Defense unless he was prepared to support him in that endeavor.[115] Shortly after coming to office, he began to question why the Army needed 100,000 soldiers in Europe to stop the Soviet Union when the Soviet Union no longer existed. In the Pacific, he questioned why South Korea and Japan could not provide more for their own defense. He also questioned the utility of keeping forces in Iceland, when their primary purpose for being there had been to track Soviet submarines.[116]

These questions caused great consternation within the Army, "some combatant commanders seemed to feel they owned the forces and assets under their command, and were loath to part with them."[117] On 10 September 2001, Rumsfeld made a speech in the Pentagon to kick-off the Department of Defense Acquisition and Logistics Excellence Week. In the speech, Rumsfeld said, there is an adversary that poses, "a serious threat to the security of the United States of America...it disrupts the defense of the United States and places the lives of men and women in uniform at risk...it is the Pentagon bureaucracy...[and its] uniformity of thought and action."[118] Accusing the military leaders and civil servants in the Pentagon of putting soldier's lives at risk is a serious accusation, one that moves beyond simple differences regarding how rapidly transformation should happen. With those words, Rumsfeld turned a professional difference of opinion into a personal attack, disillusioning the very people he would need to rely heavily upon the next day after terrorists struck the Twin Towers and the Pentagon. Nearly two years later, Rumsfeld continued to belittle military leaders, telling Lieutenant General Sanchez, "you Army guys, you have no joint experience and all of you are tied to these byzantine command structures! You don't know how to operate in a joint environment."[119]

As noted in the last chapter, Rumsfeld's experience in Lebanon led him to conclude, "Military leaders consistently hid behind narrow interpretations of the military mission and ROE constraints in order to avoid the military's larger strategic responsibility."[120] Rumsfeld believed the generals, by-in-large, did not understand what "the lethality of modern, sophisticated weapons in the hands of a well-trained military force, could do."[121] This lack of understanding was in Rumsfeld's belief, the reason for the intransigence towards transformation. In the end, the antagonistic approach Rumsfeld took with military leaders may have goaded them into transforming more rapidly than they were willing to do on their own, but it also ensured they would oppose and work against his goals whenever they could. The result was that the senior civilian leadership and the senior military leadership were so divided over the transformation issue that it affected their ability to work together to form a grand strategy for Iraq.

If the Strategy is not Working: "Americanize" it

Only if statesmen look to certain military moves and actions to produce effects that are foreign to their nature do political decisions influence operations for the worse. In the same way as a man who has not fully mastered a foreign language sometimes fails to express himself correctly, so statesmen often issue orders that defeat the purpose they are meant to serve.
—Carl von Clausewitz, *On War*[122]

The previous case study showed that when Lebanese forces failed to make progress toward achieving the outcomes desired by the US, there was a tendency to "Americanize" the effort, by adding more American training, logistics, and firepower. The previous case study concluded that these efforts may have succeeded if they were tied to a larger grand strategy, which combined political, military, and economic efforts. The same analysis can be applied to the invasion of Iraq in 2003. The US was counting on moderate Arab states, and coalition partners to immediately enter Iraq after the removal of Saddam, in order to help the liberated nation transition to a new pro-western government.[123] When it became clear in the run-up to the invasion, that the support was not going to materialize, the Office of Special Plans changed direction and decided the Coalition Provisional Authority and the US Military would have to assume control of Iraq for a minimum of a year.[124]

The problem with this change was that it was not coordinated with the military or economic efforts. Lack of coordination with the military plan is evidenced by the fact that General Franks continued to tell his subordinate commanders to assume as much risk in leaving Iraq as they had during the invasion.[125] Yet at the same time, the President, the Secretary of Defense, and the Secretary of State, told Paul Bremer he needed to prepare to be in control of Iraq for at least a year.

From an economic perspective, the US plan relied on the coalition partners to pay considerable sums of money to help Iraq rebuild and stabilize. When this did not occur, Congress approved an $18.4 billion supplemental appropriation for Iraq.[126] However, the Coalition Provisional Authority never coordinated with the US Agency for International Development on how to best spend the money. As a result, the plan to spend the money revolved almost entirely around large infrastructure projects, rather than immediate needs of the Iraqis and the things that would help bring about democracy, such as medical facilities, agricultural development, loans to small businesses, and the rebuilding of local government infrastructure that had been looted during the immediate chaos after the invasion.[127]

From a pragmatic standpoint, the US had little recourse other than to "Americanize" the strategy on the ground, once it became clear that support from moderate Arab States and coalition partners was not going to fill the void. However, from a grand strategic perspective this "Americanized" approach had little chance of initial success, because the political plan was not properly coordinated with military or economic action.

Military Roles versus Political Objectives

Prior to arriving in Iraq, Ambassador Bremer was given an unpublished RAND study, written by James Dobbins, on what was required to stabilize Iraq.[128] Dobbins extrapolated, through historical analysis, that 20 peacekeepers are needed for every 1,000 people in an occupied area.[129] For Iraq, with a population of 25 million, 500,000 peacekeepers would be required to successfully stabilize the nation.[130]

For military planners, Baghdad was the center of gravity. The 3rd ID was assigned the responsibility for capturing Baghdad, which it did through the excessive use of firepower during its Thunder Runs through the city. However, 3rd ID was ill equipped to secure the city once it had been captured. Of the 18,000 forces in 3rd ID, only 10,000 were available to conduct patrols. Out of those 10,000, only 1,200 were light infantry with the training, knowledge, equipment, and experience required to conduct stability operations.[131]

The RAND study also emphasized that when too few peacekeepers were available they tended to rely on firepower to make up for their lack of personnel. This heavy-handed tactic often results in turning the populace against the peacekeepers, thus leading to a need to revert to an even greater use of excessive force as the situation spiraled out of control.[132]

One infantry soldier from the 82nd Airborne who was sent to Baghdad to augment 3rd ID in the summer of 2003 found the excessive use of force to be astounding. "They made us all attend a course, it was really intended for loggie guys they were trying to turn into infantrymen, and I remember the instructors saying 'if there is any doubt, shoot first and then try and figure out what's going on.' I was like really? That isn't what I'd been taught [in infantry school]."[133] When the British Ambassador, John Sawers arrived in Baghdad, his first cable back to Prime Minister Tony Blair said, "the troops here [3rd ID], are tired, and are not providing the security framework needed."[134] Predictably, the good will the Iraqis initially had shown to the Americans evaporated over the summer of 2003.

Just as in Lebanon, there was a disparity between military roles and the political objective the US tried to achieve. Infantry Divisions, heavily laden with tanks and Bradley fighting vehicles, were not organized, trained, or equipped to act as peacekeeping forces. Military planners should have understood that using 3rd ID as peacekeepers in a non-permissive environment would lead to an excessive use of force that was inconsistent with the larger political objectives.

Grand Strategy

The US did not have a grand strategy in Iraq. The framework above outlined four of the primary reasons why a grand strategy was not developed. First, the government failed to recognize the importance of political reconciliation. This is evident by the fact that both political and military leaders failed to recognize the importance of political reconciliation, instead they opted to replace Saddam's regime with a Shia-dominated government. The underlying motive was to disrupt the Sunni-dominated political culture in the Middle East; something the Special Plans Office in the Pentagon knew would be a painful political process, leading to less political fighting along sectarian lines rather than reconciliation.

Second, a grand strategy could not be developed because there was conflict between the State Department and the Defense Department over how to use Ahmad Chalabi. By the time events on the ground made it evident that the US could not simply install the exiles and leave, there was no time to create a comprehensive Phase IV plan. Both Jay Garner and Paul Bremer went to Iraq under-prepared and with little official guidance from Washington. These problems may have been avoided if the National Security Council had forced the State Department and Department of Defense to settle their disputes and combine efforts to form a comprehensive grand strategy. Instead, NSPD 24 bypassed rigorous debate in the National Security Council and gave all responsibility for post-conflict Iraq to the military.[135] Unfortunately, because of the bitter disputes inside the Pentagon over transformation, Rumsfeld was no longer listening to the advice of his generals and some had stopped cooperating with him. There was no way a grand strategy could be created, or executed, within the divided Department of Defense, which was now solely in charge of post-Saddam Iraq.

Third, after Baghdad fell, and it became clear that the Iraqis would be unable to contain the looting and stop the violence, the US was forced to "Americanize" the plan using its combat forces in the place of peacekeepers, which Central Command planners had assumed would flow into Iraq from moderate Arab States and coalition partners. The President made it clear to Paul Bremer that he intended for the Coalition Provisional Authority to run Iraq for at least a year, while the infrastructure needed for a democratic Iraq was built.[136] Unfortunately, that guidance was not coordinated with the military, which continued to reduce forces in Iraq at the same time the strategy was becoming more and more "Americanized."

Finally, there was a disconnect between the roles given to the US Army and the overall political objective. The 3rd ID did not have a sufficient quantity of light infantrymen organized, trained, and equipped to stabilize Baghdad. By using tanks, Bradley Fighting Vehicles, and disproportionate force in an attempt to quell the violence, 3rd ID began to be seen as occupiers that needed to be defeated rather than liberators who needed to be supported. Ultimately, it was this loss of support that crippled the United States' mission in Iraq and ensured that the goal of creating a pro-western democratic society would take far longer and cost far more than any of the war's supporters had considered. If a grand strategy had been in place that combined all of the instruments of national power in a cohesive manner under an agreed upon political objective, the high cost paid in Iraq in terms of lives, treasure, and US prestige could have been avoided.

Notes

1. Terry H. Anderson, *Bush's Wars* (New York: Oxford University Press, 2011), 38-39. Anderson lays out five reasons why the US did not remove Saddam in 1991: fear of Iraq being partitioned by Syria, Iran and the Kurds, which could territorial issues with Turkey; The UN resolution only authorized liberating Kuwait, there was a fear that the coalition would fall apart if the US moved beyond the UN mandate. There was also a fear that the US would lose credibility with the Arab nations and be viewed as having imperialistic aims if US forces occupied Iraq. The US worried that the clear victory it had achieved in liberating Kuwait would be lost by an uncertain occupation; and finally, there was a fear that if tribal and religious hatreds were unleashed in Iraq, it could disrupt the entire region and threaten the world's access to oil.

2. Thomas Ricks, *Fiasco: The American Military Adventure in Iraq* (New York: Penguin Press, 2006), 6.

3. The Iraqi's fired at coalition aircraft no fewer than 170 times with anti-aircraft missiles and anti-aircraft artillery between 1991 and 2003. For more information, see Anthony Cordesman, *The Iraq War* (Washington DC: Praeger, 2003), 60.

4. Geoff Simons, *Future Iraq: US Policy in Reshaping the Middle East* (London: Saqi Books, 2003) 315.

5. CB20120312D0001, 4ID Political Advisor, Interview by Charles Bris-Bois, 12 March 2012, Quantico.

6. Simons, *Future Iraq,* 315.

7. Simons.

8. Cannon and Cannon, *Reagan's Disciple,* 182.

9. Cannon and Cannon.

10. George Packer, *Assassins' Gate* (New York: Farrar, Straus and Giroux, 2005), 24. France, Russia and China all opposed Operation Desert Fox for trade reasons.

11. Anderson, *Bush's Wars,* 43.

12. Anderson, 44. Zinni later stated the Arab's questions, "Shocked the hell out of me."

13. General James Jones, Memorandum for Chairman, Joint Chiefs of Staff: US Military Response in Iraq, 31 August 2001. Rumsfeld Papers, http://www.rumsfeld.com (accessed 3 March 2012).

14. General James Jones.

15. For a full analysis on Wolfowitz and Feith, see: James Bamford, *A Pretext for War: 9/11, Iraq, and the Abuse of America's Intelligence Agencies* (New York: Doubleday, 2004).

16. Seymour Hersh, *Chain of Command* (New York: HarperCollins, 2004), 173.

17. Cannon and Cannon, *Reagan's Disciple,* 189.

18. Hersh, *Chain of Command,* 138.

19. Hersh, 173.

20. Fouad Ajami, *The Foreigner's Gift: The Americans, the Arabs, and the Iraqis in Iraq* (New York: Free Press, 2006), 233.

21. Fouad Ajami, 230. Chalabi's wife is the daughter of Adel Osseiran, former Speaker of the Parliament and a leading figure in Lebanese politics. According to Ajami, the Osseirans were "one of the great notable families of the southern Shia world of Lebanon." p 230.

22. Bamford, *A Pretext for War,* 274.

23. Hersh, *Chain of Command,* 164.

24. Hersh.

25. Douglas Feith, *War and Decision: Inside the Pentagon at the Dawn of the War on Terrorism* (New York: HarperCollins, 2008), 354.

26. Douglas Feith, 355.

27. Yossef Bodansky, *The Secret History of the Iraq War* (New York, HarperCollins, 2004), 101.

28. Hersh, *Chain of Command,* 171.

29. Bodansky, *The Secret History of the Iraq War,* 86.

30. Bodansky, 165-168.

31. Tommy Franks and Malcolm McConnell, *American Soldier* (New York: HarperCollins, 2004), Chapter 9.

32. Michael Gordon, Bernard E. Trainor, and Craig Wasson, *Cobra II: The Inside Story of the Invasion and Occupation of Iraq* (New York, Pantheon, 2006), 87.

33. Cordesman, *The Iraq War,* 60.

34. Bodansky, *The Secret History of the Iraq War,* 58.

35. Micah Zenko, "Foregoing Limited Force: The George W. Bush Administration's Decision not to Attack Ansar Al-Islam," *Journal of Strategic Studies* 32, no. 4 (2009): 615-649. From Abstract: "In 2002, a terrorist group, Ansar al-Islam, operating out of a camp in Khurmal, northeast Iraq, was reportedly developing cyanide gas, toxic poisons, and ricin for potential use against Europe and the United States. The Joint Chiefs of Staff unanimously supported, and formally presented to the White House, a military operation to destroy the Ansar camp." Bodansky, *The Secret History of the Iraq War,* 51.

36. Bodansky.

37. Rumsfeld, *Known and Unknown,* 446. Prime Minister Tony Blair also objected to using the ricin found in Manchester as a reason for attacking Iraq, because the evidence clearly linked the ricin and the terrorist to Yasser Arafat and the Palestinian Authority. Blair did not want to undermine the peace process by implicating Arafat or disclose the use of Israeli intelligence in uncovering the plot. See Bodansky, *The Secret History of the Iraq War,* 51-55, for further information.

38. To see a full descriptions of V Corps and the 1st Marine Expeditionary Force, their planning and their actions during the initial invasion see Gordon et al., Cobra II, Chapters 6-11; Franks and McConnell, *American Soldier,* Chapter 9-12.

39. Cordesman, *The Iraq War,* 60.

40. Franks and McConnell, *American Soldier,* 515.

41. Franks and McConnell, 501-503.

42. Cordesman, *The Iraq War,* 159.

43. Gordon et al., *Cobra II,* Chapter 19.

44. Franks and McConnell, *American Soldier,* 523.

45. Gordon et al., *Cobra II,* 402.

46. The four phases of military operations are defined as: Phase 1. Planning, Phase II. Preparation, Phase III. Combat Operations, and Phase IV. Stability/Humanitarian/Civil Operations.

47. CB20120312F0001, ORHA Planner, Interview by Charles Bris-Bois, 14 March 2012, Washington, DC.

48. CB201120312F0001, ORHA Planner.

49. CB20120312C0001, ORHA Official, Interview.

50. CB20120410B0001, ORHA Officer. Interview by, Charles Bris-Bois, 10 April 2012, Fort Leavenworth.

51. Gordon Rudd, *Reconstructing Iraq: Regime Change, Jay Garner, and the ORHA Story* (Lawrence, KS: University Press of Kansas, 2011) 1.

52. Gordon Rudd, 2.

53. By far the most in-depth analysis of the Office of Reconstruction and Humanitarian Assistance was done by the in-house historian for the organization, Dr. Gordon Rudd. See Rudd, Reconstructing Iraq: Regime Change, Jay Garner, and the ORHA Story. See also Packer, The Assassins' Gate, Chapter 4; Gordon et al., *Cobra II,* Chapter 23.

54. Rudd, *Reconstructing Iraq,* Chapter 6.

55. The two Kurdish leaders were Massoud Barzani and Jalal Talabani. The two exiles from London were Ahmed Chalabi and Ayad Allawi. The Sunni was Naser Chaderchi and the Shias from Iran were Ibrihim al-Jaafari and Abdul Aziz Hakim. From Rudd, *Reconstructing Iraq,* 322.

56. Gordon et al., *Cobra II,* 469.

57. Gordon et al., 203. The CIA was of little use to Garner or the military in the opening month of the war, as Michael Gordon explains, Army and Marine Commander's faith in the Agency was shaken by their poor performance in the run to Baghdad. "In Iraq [unlike Afghanistan], the CIA had few contacts in the ruthlessly controlled regime of Saddam Hussein."

58. Packer, *The Assassins' Gate,* 144. Although, Garner had been told from the very beginning that he would be replaced by an US Embassy Ambassador as soon as the humanitarian relief was complete, he did not expect to be replaced so soon.

59. CB20120312F0001, ORHA Planner, Interview.

60. Paul Bremer, *My Year in Iraq: The Struggle to Build a Future of Hope* (New York: Threshold Editions, 2006), 12.

61. Bremer.

62. Bremer.

63. Bodansky, *The Secret History of the Iraq War,* 398. The Bush administration was also under pressure from Arab allies who demanded that the future

leader of Iraq must be Sunni or their own regimes would be in danger from radical Shiites they ruled. Unwilling to work with the Sunnis in Iraq, an early Bush administrations solution was to pursue a plan that called for turning Iraq into a constitutional monarchy with a Hashmite King and Ahmed Chalabi as the Prime Minister.

64. Bodansky, 43.

65. Bodansky.

66. The strong objections to the de-Baathification policy are discussed in Rudd, *Reconstructing Iraq,* 311-315, 321-324.

67. Bremer, *My Year in Iraq,* 41; Rudd, *Reconstructing Iraq,* 321. Rudd recounts the 16 May press conference announcing General Order 1, during which Bremer is quoted as saying, "We are prepared to accept that the policy will result in some temporary inefficiency in the administration of the government."

68. Bremer, *My Year in Iraq,* 41.

69. Gordon et al., *Cobra II,* 486.

70. Ricardo Sanchez and Don T. Phillips, *Wiser in Battle: A Soldier's Story* (New York: HarperCollins, 2008), 180-181.

71. Anderson, *Bush's Wars,* 150.

72. CB20120312F0001, ORHA Planner, Interview. It is not clear that the V Corps staff would have worked any better with Ambassador Bremmer than Sanchez's staff did. The problem was that roles and responsibilities were not clearly defined. Although Bremer believed he was in charge, he was never given the authority to direct the military.

73. Sanchez and Phillips, *Wiser in Battle: A Soldier's Story,* 194.

74. CB20120312F0001, ORHA Planner, Interview. Although it must be noted that this was just one of many reasons why the insurgency grew in the summer of 2003. It is also important to note that 1st Armored Division did not have a tremendous amount of Middle East experience and had just arrived in theater. The loss of team cohesion was far more damaging than the loss experience, simply because 1st Armored Division did not have a tremendous amount of experience in the Middle East.

75. Gordon et al., *Cobra II,* 461.

76. CB20120312C0001, ORHA Official, Interview.

77. Ricks, Fiasco, 110.

78. Ricks, 482.

79. CB20120328H0001, Retired Senior British Officer, Interview by Charles Bris-Bois, 28 March 2012, United Kingdom.

80. Bremer, *My Year in Iraq,* 54-56.

81. Bremer, 54.

82. Bremer, 57.

83. Ricks, Fiasco, 116.

84. Hallenbeck, Military Force as an Instrument of US Foreign Policy.

85. Condoleezza Rice, Principle Committee Review of Iraq Policy Paper, October 29, 2002, Rumsfeld Papers, http://www.rumsfeld.com (accessed 3 March 2012).

86. CB20120312F0001, ORHA Planner Interview.

87. Weisberg, *The Bush Tragedy,* 201.

88. Cannon and Cannon, *Reagan's Disciple,* 150.

89. Packer, *Assassins' Gate,* 120.

90. CB20120410B0001, ORHA Officer, Interview.

91. Packer, *Assassins' Gate,* 120.

92. Sanchez, *Wiser in Battle,* 171.

93. Rudd, *Reconstructing Iraq,* 93.

94. CB20120312D0001, 4ID Political Advisor, Interview by Charles Bris-Bois, 12 March 2012, Quantico.

95. Weisberg, *The Bush Tragedy,* 203.

96. Cannon and Cannon, *Reagan's Disciple,* 191.

97. Cannon and Cannon.

98. James Mann, *Rise of the Vulcans: the History of Bush's War Cabinet* (New York: Viking, 2004), 27.

99. Bamford, *A Pretext for War,* 276.

100. Bamford.

101. Packer, *Assassins' Gate,* 76.

102. Packer.

103. Office of the Secretary of Defense Policy, Iraqi Interim Authority Implementation Concept—Summary, 30 March 2003. Rumsfeld Papers, http://www.rumsfeld.com (accessed 3 March 2012).

104. Office of the Secretary of Defense Policy.

105. CB20120312D0001, 4ID Political Advisor, Interview by Charles Bris-Bois, 12 March 2012, Quantico.

106. Office of the Secretary of Defense Policy, Iraqi Interim Authority Implementation Concept—Summary.

107. Office of the Secretary of Defense Policy.

108. Hersh, *Chain of Command,* 166.

109. Feith, *War and Decision,* 449.

110. Hersh, *Chain of Command,* 167.

111. Hersh, *Chain of Command,* 165.

112. Rudd, *Reconstructing Iraq*, 68-73, 112. The Future of Iraq Project sought to bring all of the exile groups together and discuss pertinent issues regarding post-Saddam Iraq. The group, divided into 17 working groups, met several times over a 6 month period. Warrick produced a 1,000 page study summarizing the conclusions of those working groups.

113. Gordon et al., *Cobra II,* 159. Initially, the Pentagon rejected all seven of the State Department's ambassadorial-level officials. When Powell threatened to pull all State Department support from the Department of Defense, the Pentagon relented allowing everyone except Warrick to join ORHA.

114. Rudd, *Reconstructing Iraq,* 130.

115. Cannon and Cannon, *Reagan's Disciple,* 206; Rumsfeld, *Known and Unknown,* 283.

116. Rumsfeld, *Known and Unknown,* 302-303.

117. Rumsfeld.

118. Rumsfeld, 333.

119. Sanchez, *Wiser in Battle,* 167.

120. Hallenbeck, *Military Force as and Instrument,* 143.

121. Hallenbeck, 146.

122. Howard and Paret, *On War,* 608.

123. Rumsfeld, *Known and Unknown,* 31.

124. CB20120312F0001, ORHA Planner, Interview. See discussion above on political reconciliation.

125. Sanchez, *Wiser in Battle,* 168.

126. James Stephenson, Losing the Golden Hour (Washington DC: Potomac Books, 2007), 5.

127. James Stevenson, 89.

128. Bremer, *My Year in Iraq,* 10.

129. "Nation-Building: Lessons Learned," Memorandum from Ambassador Bremer to Secretary Rumsfeld, 4 May 2003, Rumsfeld Papers, http://www.rumsfeld.com (accessed March 3, 2012).

130. "Nation-Building: Lessons Learned," Rumsfeld Papers.

131. Gordon et al., Cobra II, 469. Even if the decision had been made to put a majority of the 18,000 troops in 3rd ID on the streets, it would have been logistically impossible. The entire division only had a few hundred sets of body armor.

132. James Dobbins, America's Role in Nation-Building: from Germany to Iraq (Santa Monica: RAND, 2003), 153.

133. CB20120510A0001, Infantry Officer, Interview by Charles Bris-Bois, 10 May 2012, Fort Leavenworth.

134. Gordon et al., *Cobra II,* 472.

135. CB20120312C0001, ORHA Official. Interview.

136. Bremer, *My Year in Iraq,* 41-43.

Chapter 6
Conclusion

Theory

Chapter 2 began with a discussion of Clausewitz's struggle to reconcile the multiple types of war he found in his analysis of history into a single theory of war. Using the analogy of weapons, Clausewitz said absolute war was like a "terrible battle-sword that a man needs both hands and his entire strength to wield, and with which he strikes home once and no more."[1] History, however, revealed another type of war, one in which the mighty sword became merely an instrument, "a light, handy rapier—sometimes just a foil for the exchange of thrusts, faints and parries."[2] To reconcile these contradictions, Clausewitz determined that policy was the instrument governments used to limit and expand wars. In Book Eight, Chapter Six, of *On War* it states, "as policy becomes more ambitious and vigorous, so will war."[3] Clausewitz further states, "only if war is looked at in this way does the unity reappear, only then can we see that all wars are things of the same nature."[4] In many ways, Clausewitz's "policy" is a simplified expression of what we call grand strategy today. As the Prussian General explained, policy represented, "all the interest of the state," policy, "unifies and reconciles all aspects of the internal administration ... and is representative of all interests of the community."[5]

However, as discussed in Chapter 2, Clausewitz failed to admit that there were times when the internal interests of the state could not be unified or reconciled, or that states may have competing and contradictory interests. This is why Liddell Hart's expansion of Clausewitz's themes is so important. Liddell Hart interpreted Clausewitz's policy as "the object of war, what is to be achieved," while grand strategy was policy in action, "The [coordination and direction] of all the resources of a nation... towards the attainment of the political object of the war—the goal defined by the fundamental policy."[6]

Walter Russell Mead and Eliot Cohen use historical analysis of American Foreign Policy to show that coordination and direction of all the resources of the nation in a unified manner has never been achieved.[7] There have always been contradictions, tensions, and uneasy compromises in the formulation of US grand strategy. The presence of these conflicts can be attributed to the differences between the schools of thought that have evolved within US strategic planning circles. A few of these dominant characteristics revolve around the military's preference for excessively neat civil-military relations, precluding diplomats and generals from working hand-in-hand to craft holistic, yet nuanced strategies. This lack of cooperation leads to conflict over what to do and how to do it. Finally, historical analysis shows that while sorting through these complexities and tensions, America's Jeffersonian preference for overwhelming firepower and direct violent assault, takes the lead and often undermines the very goals the US is trying to achieve.

The two case studies in this paper, Lebanon 1982 to 1984, and Iraq 2003, demonstrated the desire and the need for the US to wield the rapier rather than the terrible sword. However, the US never had a policy or grand strategy that unified and reconciled all the internal aspects of the administration. The Department of Defense and Department of State struggled over how to implement the President's guidance and the plans they formulated were at best filled with contradictions, tensions, and uneasy compromises. When plans failed in both Lebanon and Iraq, the US, as it has shown a proclivity to do, resorted to overwhelming firepower and direct violent assault, undermining the very goals it was trying to achieve.

Lebanon

The contradictions, tensions, and uneasy compromises that were made in the planning and execution of the US Military's intervention in Lebanon in 1982 to 1984 fit into the larger pattern of US Foreign Policy Cohen and Russell lay out. It was clear early in the dispute that military force would have to be combined with diplomacy in a well-timed and coherent fashion in order to achieve the political reconciliation, upon which the entire US strategy rested.

However, this did not occur due to disputes between the Department of Defense, the Department of State, and the National Security Council. To borrow Clausewitz's analogy, Secretary of State Shultz sought to use the military as a rapier, applying closely coordinated military action to strengthen what was primarily a diplomatic effort. Secretary of Defense Weinberger did not believe the military should be used in such a fashion and therefore, he fought continuously for strict ROE that severely limited how the military could be used. This conflict can clearly be seen in National Security Presidential Directive103, which codified the differences between State and Defense, rather than unifying and reconciling their internal disputes.

As a result of NSPD103, the Department of Defense reluctantly agreed to the State Department's demands to "Americanize" the effort by increasing the use of firepower. The ROE defined in NSPD103, however, created conditions that did not allow for well-timed and coordinated military action when the diplomats needed it to strengthen their positions. Instead, it often took days to get approval necessary for the application of firepower. The uncoordinated use of firepower and diplomacy led to the perception that the US was no longer a non-partisan player. The use of naval gunfire to shell the Shouf and Syrian positions, and the training the Marines provided to the LAF, undermined the US policy of wanting to be viewed as an even-handed negotiator in the peace process. Ultimately, this contributed to the conditions under which the factions felt justified in attacking the US Forces.

Had the Department of Defense, Department of State, and the National Security Council worked together to formulate a grand strategy, it is not possible to determine whether the US would have achieved its political objectives. The issues are too complex and there is simply no way to predict in hindsight how the opposing forces would have reacted to a coordinated US grand strategy. However, it is entirely reasonable to assume that the Marines would not have been forced into ROE that restricted them almost entirely to the International Airport and made them an easy target both to shelling from the Shouf and to terrorist attacks. It is also safe to assume that the escalation in military force that culminated in the shelling of Syrian positions by the USS New Jersey's 16-inch guns, with no discernable objective other than retribution, would not have occurred. Finally, a coordinated grand strategy would have gone a long way in preventing the situation the US found itself in 1984, facing two unfavorable outcomes. The US was forced to decide whether to escalate the war and risk greater regional conflict including possible direct confrontation with the Soviets or withdraw under the perception that the Syrians and Islamic militants had forced the US out of Lebanon.

Iraq

As in Lebanon, disputes between the Department of State and the Department of Defense prevented the US from formulating, or executing, a grand strategy that would have coordinated and directed resources towards the attainment of the political objectives. These disputes revolved primarily around Ahmed Chalabi and the role external opposition groups should play in deposing Saddam and running a post-Saddam Iraq. In addition, there were strong philosophical differences between State and Defense, differences that Mead defined as the differences between Hamiltonians, Wilsonians, Jeffersonians, and Jacksonians.

The State Department under Powell was heavily slanted toward the Jeffersonians, distrustful of alliances with unsavory partners and the wisdom of attempting to spread democracy. In contrast, the Department of

Defense, led by neoconservatives, favored a combination of the Wilson and Jackson schools of thought. From Jackson, the Department of Defense took the view that Iraq and any other state, which sponsored terrorism and sought weapons of mass destruction, had to be defeated militarily. Yet in a very Wilsonian way, the neoconservatives represented by Feith and Wolfowitz in the Pentagon, sought to change the dynamics of the Middle East by installing a pro-western Shia led democratic government in Iraq that would change the balance of power and ultimately lead to the spread of democracy throughout the region.[8]

These disputes became so contentious that the two departments were unable to form a unified and reconciled plan for Phase IV operations. In theory, the interagency process, under the direction of the National Security Council, should have reconciled the differences between the departments. However, the process was cut short by NSPD 24, which ended interagency debate by giving full control of post-invasion Iraq to the Department of Defense.

With the Office of the Secretary of Defense in full control of post-Saddam Iraq, Feith, the Undersecretary of Defense for Policy, was able to recommend last-minute, uncoordinated changes regarding the structure of the new Iraqi Government to Bremer. In fairness, these changes were required in late March and early April of 2003, when it became clear that Chalabi and the exiles did not have popular support among the Iraqi people to govern the country. The fact that the ideas originated in the Office of the Under Secretary of Defense for Policy contradicts the popular narrative that Bremer was making decisions on his own without Pentagon guidance. The decision to change from a quick handover to a long term occupation was made in April of 2003 as US Forces raced to Baghdad. As the evidence in chapter 5 showed, The Office of the Secretary of Defense convinced the President and the principals on the National Security Council that this decision was required to prepare Iraq for democracy.

This change gave Bremer and the Coalition Provisional Authority the mandate to carry out harsh de-Baathification rules and disband the Iraqi security forces. However, because the change in direction happened literally while US Forces were advancing on Baghdad, there was no time to coordinate the military, economic, or information campaigns required to create a secure environment in which Iraq could be prepared for democracy.

If grand strategy is the coordination and direction of all the resources of a nation, than clearly the US did not have one in Iraq. Primarily because the government failed to direct and coordinate the nation's immense resources, the Americans found themselves in control of Iraq with too few forces. The forces they had were not organized, trained, or equipped properly to conduct security operations. The heavy-handed tactics used by the US Forces in an attempt to quell the violence and end the chaos undermined the strategic message that the Americans were in Iraq to help. These actions inadvertently provided justification for those that opposed the US to attack American Forces.

Again, had the Department of Defense, Department of State, and the National Security Council worked together to formulate a grand strategy for Iraq, it is not possible to determine whether the US would have been able to avoid the violence and disintegration of Iraqi society that started in 2003 and lasted until the Surge in 2007. The issues are too complex and there is simply no way to predict in hindsight how the opposing forces would have reacted to a coordinated US grand strategy. However, it is entirely reasonable to assume that the plan to switch from liberation to occupation would not have been formulated at the last minute, while US Forces were racing to Baghdad. It is also highly probable that the tremendous turnover of organizations and personnel that took place during the summer of 2003 would not have occurred simultaneously. Finally, had there been a unified grand strategy, one can safely assume the de-Baathification order and the order to disband the Iraqi security forces would have been debated by the National Security Council. If still deemed appropriate, the orders would have been issued in a manner that allowed for sufficient military force to mitigate the inherent risks.

Ultimately, the question this paper answered was not, "would a grand strategy have ensured successful achievement of the political objectives in Lebanon and Iraq?" The question was, "Did the US have a grand strategy when viewed through the prism of Lebanon in 1982 and Iraq in 2003?" The two case studies and the framework used which examined four critical factors in determining if a grand strategy existed, suggests the answer is emphatically no.

Notes

1. Howard and Paret, *On War*, 606.
2. Howard and Paret.
3. Howard and Paret.
4. Howard and Paret.
5. Howard and Paret, 107.
6. Liddell Hart, *Strategy,* 322.
7. Mead, *Special Providence*, 28-29.
8. Mead, *Special Providence,* Chapters 5, 6 and 7.

Glossary

ID	Infantry Division
LAF	Lebanese Armed Forces
MAU	Marine Amphibious Unit
NSPD	National Security Presidential Directive
PLO	Palestinian Liberation Organization
ROE	Rules of Engagement
UN	United Nations
US	United States

Bibliography

Interviews

Fort Leavenworth

CB20120510A0001, Infantry Officer. Interview by Charles Bris-Bois, Fort Leavenworth, KS, 10 May 2012.

CB20120410B0001, ORHA Officer. Interview by Charles Bris-Bois, Fort Leavenworth, KS, 10 April 2012.

Marine Corps Base Quantico

CB20120312C0001, ORHA Official. Interview by, Charles Bris-Bois, Fort Leavenworth, KS, 8 March 2012.

CB20120312D0001, 4ID Political Advisor. Interview by, Charles Bris-Bois, Fort Leavenworth, KS, 8 March 2012.

CB20120313E0001, CIA Analyst. Interview by, Charles Bris-Bois, Fort Leavenworth, KS, 13 March 2012.

Washington DC

CB20120312F0001, ORHA Planner. Interview by Charles Bris-Bois, Fort Leavenworth, KS, 14 March 2012.

United Kingdom

CB20120327G0001, Senior British Official. Interview by Charles Bris-Bois, Fort Leavenworth, KS, 27 March 2012.

CB20120328H0001, Retired Senior British Officer. Interview by Charles Bris-Bois, Fort Leavenworth, KS, 28 March 2012.

CB20120329I0001, Retired Senior British Officer. Interview by Charles Bris-Bois, Fort Leavenworth, KS, 29 March 2012.

Books

Ajami, Fouad. *The Foreigner's Gift: The Americans, the Arabs, and the Iraqis in Iraq.* New York: Free Press, 2006.

Allawi, Ali A. *The Occupation of Iraq: Winning the War, Losing the Peace.* New Haven, CT: Yale University Press, 2007.

Anderson, Terry H. *Bush's Wars.* New York: Oxford University Press, 2011.

Bamford, James. *A Pretext for War: 9/11, Iraq, and the Abuse of America's Intelligence Agencies.* New York: Doubleday Publishing, 2004.

Best, Jr., Richard A. *The National Security Council: An Organizational Assessment.* Washington, DC: Congressional Research Service, 2009.

Bodansky, Yossef. *The Secret History of the Iraq War.* New York: ReganBooks, 2004.

Bremer, Paul. *My Year in Iraq: The Struggle to Build a Future of Hope.* New York: Threshold Editions, 2006.

Cannon, Lou, and Carl M. Cannon. *Reagan's Disciple: George W. Bush's Troubled Quest for a Presidential Legacy.* New York: PublicAffairs, 2008.

Cerami, Joseph R., James F. Holcomb, and Army War College. *US Army War College Guide to Strategy. Carlisle Barracks,* PA: Strategic Studies Institute, US Army War College, 2001.

Cerami, Joseph R., Robert H. Dorff, Matthew H. Harber, eds. *National Security Reform 2010: A Mid-Term Assessment.* Carlisle Barracks, PA: Strategic Studies Institute, US Army War College, 2011.

Clausewitz, Carl von, *On War.* Edited Beatrice Heuser. Oxford: Oxford University Press, 2008.

Cohen, Eliot. "The strategy of innocence? The United States, 1920-1945." In *The Making of Strategy: Rules, States, and War,* edited by Williamson Murray, MacGregor Knox, and Alvin Bernstein 428-465. New York: Cambridge University Press, 1994.

Collelo, Thomas, ed. *Lebanon, a Country Study.* United States: 1989.

Collins, John M. *Grand Strategy: Principles and Practices.* Annapolis, MD: Naval Institute Press, 1973.

Cordesman, Anthony. *The Iraq War.* Washington DC: Praeger, 2003.

Davis, M. Thomas. *40km into Lebanon: Israel's 1982 Invasion.* Washington, DC: National Defense University Press, 1987.

Drew, Col Dennis M. and Dr. Donald M. Snow. *Making Strategy: An Introduction to National Security Processes and Problems.* Maxwell, AL: Air University Press, 1988.

Dobbins, James. *America's Role in Nation-Building from Germany to Iraq.* Santa Monica, CA: RAND Corporation, 2003.

Echevarria, Antulio Joseph. *Clausewitz and Contemporary War.* New York: Oxford University Press, 2007.

Feith, Douglas J. *War and Decision: Inside the Pentagon at the Dawn of the War on Terrorism.* New York: HarperCollins Publishers, 2008.

Fishel, John T. *Civil Military Operations in the New World.* Westport, CT: Praeger, 1997.

Frank, Benis M. *US Marines in Lebanon, 1982-1984.* Washington, DC: Government Printing Office, 1987.

Franks, Tommy, and Malcolm McConnell. *American Soldier.* New York: Regan Books, 2005.

Gabriel, Richard A. *Operation Peace for Galilee: The Israeli-PLO War in Lebanon.* New York: Hill and Wang, 1984.

Geraghty, Timothy J. *Peacekeepers at War: Beirut 1983: The Marine Commander Tells His Story.* Washington, DC: Potomac Books, 2009.

Goldgeier, James M. *Not Whether but when: The US Decision to Enlarge NATO.* Washington, DC: Brookings Institution Press, 1999.

Gordon, Michael R., Bernard E. Trainor, and Craig Wasson. *Cobra II: The Inside Story of the Invasion and Occupation of Iraq.* Random House Audio, 2006.

Hallenbeck, Ralph A. *Military Force as an Instrument of US Foreign Policy: Intervention in Lebanon, August 1982-February 1984.* New York: Praeger, 1991.

Hammel, Eric M. *The Root: The Marines in Beirut, August 1982-February 1984.* St Paul: Zenith, 2005.

Hersh, Seymour. *Chain of Command.* New York: HarperCollins, 2004.

Howard, Michael Eliot, and Peter Paret, eds. *On War.* Princeton, NJ: Princeton University Press, 1984.

Huchthausen, Peter A. *America's Splendid Little Wars: A Short History of US Military Engagements, 1975-2000.* New York: Viking, 2003.

Laffin, John. *The War of Desperation: Lebanon 1982-85.* London: Osprey, 1985.

Liddell Hart, B. H. *Strategy,* 2nd ed. London: Meridian Printing, 1991.

Mackey, Sandra. *Lebanon: Death of a Nation.* Chicago: Congdon & Weed, 1989.

Mann, James. *Rise of the Vulcans: The History of Bush's War Cabinet.* New York: Viking, 2004.

Mead, Walter Russell. *Power, Terror, Peace, and War: America's Grand Strategy in a World at Risk.* New York: Knopf, 2004.

———. *Special Providence: American Foreign Policy and how it Changed the World.* New York: Knopf, 2001.

Murray, Williamson, MacGregor Knox, and Alvin H. Bernstein. *The Making of Strategy: Rulers, States, and War.* Cambridge: Cambridge University Press, 1994.

Nuechterlein, Donald. *America Overcommitted: United States National Interests in the 1980s.* Lexington: University of Kentucky Press, 1985.

Odeh, B. J. *Lebanon: Dynamics of Conflict: A Modern Political History.* London: Zed Books, 1985.

Packer, George. *The Assassins' Gate: America in Iraq.* New York: Farrar, Straus and Giroux, 2005.

Paret, Peter, Gordon Alexander Craig, and Felix Gilbert. *Makers of Modern Strategy: From Machiavelli to the Nuclear Age.* Princeton, NJ: Princeton University Press, 1986.

Ricks, Thomas E. *Fiasco: The American Military Adventure in Iraq.* New York: Penguin Press, 2006.

Rudd, Gordon W. *Reconstructing Iraq: Regime Change, Jay Garner, and the ORHA Story.* Lawrence, KS: University Press of Kansas, 2011.

Rumsfeld, Donald. *Known and Unknown: A Memoir.* New York: Sentinel, 2011.

Sanchez, Ricardo S., and Don T. Phillips. *Wiser in Battle: A Soldier's Story.* New York: Harpercollins, 2008.

Shultz, George Pratt. *Turmoil and Triumph: My Years as Secretary of State.* New York: Maxwell Macmillan Canada, 1993.

Simons, Geoff L. *Future Iraq: US Policy in Reshaping the Middle East.* London: Saqi, 2003.

Snider, Don M. *The National Security Strategy: Documenting Strategic Vision.* Carlisle Barracks, PA: Strategic Studies Institute, US Army War College, 1995.

Snider, Don M., and John A. Nagl. *The National Security Strategy: Documenting Strategic Vision.* Carlisle, PA: US Army War College, 2001.

Spiller, Roger J. *Not War, but Like War: The American Intervention in Lebanon.* Fort Leavenworth, KS: Combat Studies Institute, 1981.

Stephenson, James. *Losing the Golden Hour: An Insider's View of Iraq's Reconstruction.* Washington, DC: Potomac Books, 2007.

Strachan, Hew. *Clausewitz's on War: A Biography.* New York: Distributed by Publishers Group West, 2007.

Weigley, Russell F. *The American Way of War: A History of United States Military Strategy and Policy.* Bloomington: Indiana University Press, 1977.

Weinberger, Caspar W. *Fighting for Peace: Seven Critical Years in the Pentagon.* New York: Warner Books, 1990.

Weinberger, Caspar W., and Gretchen Roberts. *In the Arena: A Memoir of the 20th Century.* Lanham, MD: National Book Network, 2001.

Weisberg, Jacob. *The Bush Tragedy.* New York: Random House, 2008.

Willis, Jeffrey R. *Employment of US Marines in Lebanon 1982-1984.* Fort Leavenworth, KS: US Army Command and General Staff College, 1992.

Yates, Lawrence A. *US Military's Experience in Stability Operations, 1789-2005.* Fort Leavenworth, KS: Combat Studies Institute Press, 2006.

Other Sources

Foster, Gregory D. McNair Paper 27. *In Search of Post-Cold War Security Structure.* Washington, DC: National Defense University, Institute for National Strategic Studies, February 1994.

Gaddis, John L. "What is Grand Strategy." Duke University, Keynote address for a conference on "American Grand Strategy after War," 2009.

Marine Corps University, Gray Research Center Archives

Geraghty, Col Timothy J., USMC. Interview by Benis M. Frank, on board USS Iwo Jima, 21 November 1983. Benis M. Frank Papers. Gray Research Center Archives. Marine Corps University Library, Quantico, VA.

Mead, Col James M. USMC. Interview by Benis M. Frank, Camp Geiger, 13 January 1983. Benis M. Frank Papers. Gray Research Center Archives. Marine Corps University Library, Quantico, VA.

———. Interview by Benis M. Frank, Marine Corps Head Quarters, 5 May 1984. Benis M. Frank Papers. Gray Research Center Archives. Marine Corps University Library, Quantico, VA.

———. Speech to Naval War College, 14 September 1983. Benis M. Frank Papers, Gray Research Center Archives, Marine Corps University Library, Quantico, VA.

———. Marine Corps Oral History Program Interview. Interviewed by Benis M. Frank, 23 May 1983.

Rumsfeld Papers

Jones, General James. Memorandum for Chairman, Joint Chiefs of Staff: US Military Response in Iraq, 31 August 2001. Rumsfeld Papers, http://www.rumsfeld.com (accessed 3 March 2012).

Memorandum from Ambassador Bremer to Secretary Rumsfeld. "Nation-Building: Lessons Learned." 4 May 2003, Rumsfeld Papers. http://www.rumsfeld.com (accessed 3 March 2012).

Office of the Secretary of Defense Policy. *Iraqi Interim Authority Implementation Concept—Summary,* 30 March 2003. Rumsfeld Papers. http://www.rumsfeld.com (accessed 3 March 2012).

Rice, Condoleezza. *Principle Committee Review of Iraq Policy Paper, 29 October 2002.* Rumsfeld Papers. http://www.rumsfeld.com (accessed 3 March 2012).

Government Documents

Joint Chiefs of Staff. Joint Publication (JP) 1, *Doctrine for the Armed Forces of the United States.* Washington, DC: Government Printing Office, 2007, Incorporating Change 1, 20 March 2009.

Journals

Hahn, Peter L. "Securing the Middle East: The Eisenhower Doctrine of 1957." *Presidential Studies Quarterly* 36, no. 1 (2006): 38-47.

LaFeber, Walter. "The Bush Doctrine." *Diplomatic History 26,* no. 4 (2002): 543-58.

Singh, Michael. "Making the NSC Work." *The American Interest 5,* no. 2 (2009): 78.

Zenko, Micah. "Foregoing Limited Force: The George W. Bush Administration's Decision Not to Attack Ansar Al-Islam." *Journal of Strategic Studies* 32, no. 4 (2009): 615-49.

Internet Sources

Bush, President George W. "Address to a Joint Session of Congress and the American People," 20 September, 2001. georgewbush-whitehouse. archives.gov/news/releases/2001/09/20010920-8 html (accessed 15 April 2012).

Drezner, Daniel W. "Values, Interests, and American Grand Strategy." danieldrezner.com/research/leffler.pdf (accessed 7 April 2012).

Kiefer, Todd. "Competition, War and Transformation: Interagency Framework for Operational Planning and Force Development." Briefing on 2 June 2004. www.au.af.mil/au/awc/awcgate/jcs/competition.ppt/ (accessed 1 March 2012).

Marcella, Gabriel. *Affairs of State: The Interagency and National Security* (Washington, DC: National Strategic Studies Institute, December 2008. StrategicStudiesInstitute.army mil/pdffiles/Pub896.pdf (accessed 15 March 2012).

www.ingramcontent.com/pod-product-compliance
Lightning Source LLC
Chambersburg PA
CBHW081841280526
45789CB00007B/2527